G000146324

DISRUPTED

STRATEGY FOR EXPONENTIAL CHANGE

LIMITED AUSTRALIAN EDITION

LARRY QUICK AND **DAVID PLATT**

WITH **KRISTIN VAN VLOTEN**

Foreword by Todd Davies, FCA PFIIA CRMA MAICD

resilient futures media

WWW.RESILIENTFUTURES.COM

RESILIENT FUTURES MEDIA
Victoria, Australia

First published by Resilient Futures Media as a limited edition in September 2015

Cover and layout design by Iskon Design, New York
ISBN: 978-0-9943769-0-9
Printed in Australia
RFMedia@resilientfutures.com

CONTENTS

AUTHOR'S DISCLAIMER

We would like to stress that we have no personal, professional or financial links with the organizations (e.g. Apple, Whole Foods, Airbnb, Tesla, Netflix, and Uber) used as examples in this book. All professional relationships have been stated when used as cases.

We would also like to add that we are not promoting use of or investment in any of these organizations, or implying that they will avoid disruption in the future.

It is our belief that all organizations are subject to disruption. Even a disruptor will more than likely be disrupted in the future. They, like you, will have to answer the same question: "Do we leverage creative disruption or fall into the same pattern of creative destruction that the organizations we once disrupted chose?

FOREWORD | By Todd Davies

FOREWORD

By Todd Davies

I had a front row seat as I watched and possibly accelerated the death of the majors in the music industry. And, then for a second time, I had a similar view as the newspaper industry went over the cliff. I'm now seeing the same pattern unfold with many (and maybe most) listed companies in Australia and have been working with some of them to help them get out in front.

For me, the early part of this century can be best described as "the great hollowing out." During this time, it seems as if companies responded year-by-year to significant change by cutting their cloth to suit until all that was left was an anaemic version of their former business, without a toehold in the future.

Examples of this "hollowing out" are so common that there is no need to name them here. You can probably list several off the top of your head. You may even work for one.

Sure, there have been some improvements to the customer experience over the years, but this period has been largely characterized by the ongoing quest for savings and bolt on acquisitions where someone else creates value and the entrepreneurial spirit is a distant memory. Risk aversion is king and genuine value creation is left to others.

While this approach has worked in the past due to barriers to entry and natural oligopolies, in a global, interconnected world this is a recipe for disaster and the death knell of our economy. The tide in corporate Australia is going out. Fast.

The reality is that value creation, particularly platform creation, is happening offshore, and by the time Australian companies get to the party in any meaningful way it will likely be too late.

After many years of focus on efficiency many large organizations (and possibly most) have a terminal disease. It's not cancer, but it may as well be. Bureaucracy and risk aversion have trumped entrepreneurship and value creation in just about everything we do. I've been guilty of this. You probably have been too.

Today, asset write-downs and redundancy costs are no longer abnormal items. They are just lag indicators that the deckchairs are being shifted on the Titanic as each organisation is being disrupted in their own way. Look at any company reporting on underlying earnings and you'll see these symptoms are widespread.

Many company directors state that they don't want a "Kodak moment" on their CVs. The fact is, they probably already have at least one. You might have one right now.

The "hollowing out" is turning the corner, but not for the best - the quickening has arrived. In many sectors there may only be one dominant player or platform. Maybe it's you. Maybe it's not. But if you don't act quickly and decisively, it will definitely be the other guy. And they'll probably be foreign owned.

If you're lucky, you're on the flat part of the disruption curve and you've got a foothold in the future. If so, there may still be time. If not, I'll be watching the "Kodak class actions" of the next decade with dismay.

But there is another way.

This book is an urgent call to action for organizations of all shapes and sizes, but more importantly it brings back the thrill of the entrepreneurial spirit and the quest to create a new and better future for you and everyone you work with. It is a cure to the malaise and something worth getting up and going to work for.

While this book can only scratch the surface of 25 years of thinking, it will start giving you new tools for getting out in front and making a difference in profound and game-changing ways.

Having worked with, learned, developed and applied various aspects of the model over the last 23 years, I can definitely vouch for this.

Before my life in corporate, in the "disruption business" we had a saying: *"Fast food. (If you're not fast, you're food)."* When disruption appears, you can either choose to eat the meal or *be* the meal. That's entirely up to you.

Clear your diary. Read this book. It may be the beginning of something exhilarating and spectacular.

Todd Davies, FCA PFIIA CRMA MAICD
Chairman
Resilient Futures

ABOUT DISRUPTED

"People don't *get* exponential."

Those words rang in my (Larry's) ears for months after I first heard them in March 1996. They were spoken in a quiet but frank tone by Nicholas Negroponte, the head of MIT's Media Lab and author of *Being Digital*.

To put Nicholas's (now twenty-year old) view of "the exponential" into context, on that day he was discussing "the move from atoms to bits", "books without pages", "smart cars", "wearable media" and "cottage TV". Sound familiar?

Twenty years ago it all sounded like science fiction. Now it's the world we live in.

Though the speculative part of Nicholas's talk was interesting, what struck me the most was his view on the speed and convergence of a whole system of change.

Today we take what he said in 1996 for granted. But are we really seeing Nicholas's "trickle that became a downpour" view of exponential change? Do we recognize it starting to exert itself as a "long beginning to a shock awakening"? Do we realize that we are ill equipped to deal with, much less leverage disruption?

Overall, we think not. Twenty years ago people didn't "get" exponential change and today too many still don't.

This will be bad news for many, but good news for the few who are already ahead of the game, leveraging exponential disruption for their own advantage.

Allow us to explain.

In 1979, depending on who you were, the advent of quartz watchmaking went by two names: the Quartz Crisis and the Quartz Revolution. Mechanical watchmakers in the storied Swiss tradition preferred to call it by the former, while Asian manufacturing upstarts heard the call of opportunity and proceeded to build a new industry.

In 1888, George Eastman founded a company that grew rich by selling cheap cameras and expensive film. The Eastman Kodak Company was responsible for the popularization of amateur photography, a technological wave that resulted in handheld cameras documenting the intimate moments of everyday life across the planet. For a time, anything worth remembering was known as a "Kodak moment." But the company that employed 145,000 people in 1988 was shedding market share like so much overexposed film by the late 1990s and early 2000s. When Kodak filed for bankruptcy in 2012, the smartphone had replaced the once-revolutionary camera as the ubiquitous technology for documenting all of those "Kodak moments".

Quartz watches and digital cameras: bad news for the old guard and good news for the upstarts.

But here's where the bad news/good news dichotomy breaks down: both quartz watches and digital photography were inside jobs. The Swiss helped pioneer quartz technology and one of Kodak's very own, Steve Sasson, invented the "filmless camera." *In 1975.* At what point did Kodak's bad news become Apple's good news? Did the Swiss miss the opportunity to take greater ownership of their own bad news? Could they have instead worked with it up until the point when it could have become very good news for their venerable industry, leading a breakthrough into an entirely new era of craftsmanship?

The dictionary defines *disruption* as "disturbances or problems that interrupt an event, activity, or process." But for some time now the word has also been used to describe the radical developments that bring new products and markets into existence. It would seem, then, that disruption is both destruction and creation. It's destruction that *becomes* creation over time. Or else it's creation that *becomes* destruction over time. Good news becoming bad news and bad news becoming good.

Uber is the world's largest taxi company and they don't own any taxis. Airbnb is the word's largest hotelier and they don't own any accommodations. Skype is one of the world's largest phone companies and they don't own any telecommunications infrastructure. Netflix is the world's largest theatre company and they don't own any cinemas. Facebook is the world's most popular media channel and they don't create content. Apple and Google are the world's largest software vendors and they don't write apps.

This is more than digital disruption. This is the deliberate squashing of conventional business models, backed by an investment sector that has moved on from just funding the next best widget, to start-ups that can successfully disrupt business models. And *quickly.*

THIS IS EXPONENTIAL DISRUPTION. IT'S BOTH BAD NEWS AND GOOD. IT'S BOTH DESTRUCTION AND CREATION.

We, the authors of *Disrupted*, are members of a network of strategic planning, risk management and systems analysis specialists called Resilient Futures. We have spent over twenty years creating a framework for strategy that is simple and agile enough to help leaders, teams, networks, and communities ride waves of disruptive change. We are strategists with experience from a multitude of industries and sectors. We have coached and consulted with organizations, businesses, and communities in order to help them achieve great things in the face of disruptive and accelerating exponential change. We're ready to share what we've learned.

We wrote this book to convince you that you're looking at very good news no matter what form of disruption is transforming your organization and industry. This message is not just for someone else in some other foresighted and agile organization. This is for you.

A banking CEO whose organization lost $2 billion USD worth of shareholder funds in the wake of the global financial crisis said: "No one could have reasonably foreseen these circumstances." We want you to know that he and his blinder-wearing ilk are wrong. By the time you have finished this book, you'll understand that it *is* possible to both foresee transformative disruptions and to leverage them for your own benefit and the benefit of the people in your organization.

Furthermore, leveraging the disruptions you've seen over the horizon is a capability, a philosophy, and a way of life that will only become more crucial with the passage of time. We are now in an "elbow" of exponential change, when the forces that have driven disruption over the course of history are converging and reaching a series of tipping points.

As these tipping points mount up, we have seen many organizations across the United States and Australia succumb to the same fatal illness our "reasonable" banking CEO suffered from. We call it M.A.D. or Managed Adaptive Decline, and it occurs when an organization or a community ignores "bad news" and then develops elegantly efficient yet ultimately futile strategies for coping with its disruptions. By "going lean" or "managing harder" they divert energy away from solutions and further exacerbate their fundamental ills. Like the proverbial frog in the pot, they accept their fate in a spirit of willful ignorance and passivity, and by the time their business model is boiling to death, it's too late to evacuate the cookware.

We believe that those who pay attention to the temperature changing underneath their feet are well positioned to win big. The opportunities in this exponentially accelerating era are immense. There is plenty of good news for disruption-leveraging individuals, organizations, and industries. We want to give you an alternative to the strategy and planning methodologies that might be steering your organization into the hot water of M.A.D. After all, you can't use the same tool that caused the damage to fix the problem. It's time to update your strategic thinking—and quickly—if you want to avoid falling into a pattern of teeth-gritting decline.

With this book, it's our intention to provide you with a simple framework for understanding your disruptions and strategically leveraging them. In other words, we want to inform you about how to treat bad news like good news. We call our framework Strategy In Action, or SiA, and it's been road-tested in a variety of settings and industries. Basically, it's an algorithm simple enough to allow you to assess conditions, make choices, and take action in the real-time of your exponentially evolving reality. To that end, this book is a guidebook to this era of exponentially accelerating changes and a toolbox for proactively leveraging those changes, rather than falling prey to their more chaotic, destructive, and demotivating effects. Above all, this book is a series of stories about people passing through the crucible of opportunity and risk with confidence and insight and coming out the other side with something of enduring value.

Chapters 1 and 2 will get you up to speed on the nature of exponential change and introduce you to SiA, our five-pronged framework—or algorithm—for leveraging disruption.

Chapters 3 to 7 will break down the five components of the SiA algorithm. Each of these chapters examines how disruption-opportunists like Apple, Whole Foods, and Tesla work in tune with their times, embodying the principles of SiA. To encourage you to continually consider how these principles apply to your experience, we have punctuated these chapters with questions meant to stimulate reflection. Finally, each of these five chapters ends with a checklist summarizing key takeaways. Taken together, they function as a master list of concepts or practices that represent your "Disruption Readiness".

Chapter 8 will send you on your way, ready to strategize on your feet and think differently about the brilliantly unprecedented future awaiting you.

This book has been twenty years in the making. We hope it provides you and many other leaders and teams with a context, instructive examples, and solutions for acting ahead of disruption. Our belief in the power of creative and collaborative people to leverage change for awe-inspiring outcomes underpins the entire text. We hope this belief is contagious. There is plenty of risk on the horizon but you have so much cause for confidence. After all, many others have trodden this path before you.

To take the first step, ask yourself, "Do I actually get exponential?"

Then ask, "What are our disruptors, and how are we going to leverage them to generate sustainable value?" Then celebrate the good news, whatever it is.

Larry Quick and David Platt

CHAPTER 1 | Welcome to the Wake-Up

LIVING IN AN EXPONENTIALLY ACCELERATING AGE

WHAT IT MEANS TO LIVE IN AN AGE OF DISRUPTION. HOW EXPONENTIAL CHANGE WORKS, WHICH FACTORS ARE DRIVING IT, AND HOW A NEW PHILOSOPHY OF CHANGE CAN HELP US TO BETTER NAVIGATE IT.

" *WE ARE THINKING ABOUT THE FUTURE IN A LOCAL AND LINEAR FASHION...TODAY WE LIVE IN A WORLD THAT IS GLOBAL AND EXPONENTIAL...THE WORLD IS NOT CHANGING CENTURY TO CENTURY OR DECADE TO DECADE. IT IS CHANGING YEAR TO YEAR.* "

Peter Diamandis

THE ELBOW

Imagine you meet a very wealthy man. He wants to hire you for a job that will take thirty days. It's not difficult work, but it's an entire month of your life. You ask him: What are the payment terms?

"You have two choices," he replies. "You can either take one million dollars now, or you can drive to my house every day to collect your payment. If you choose the second option, you get paid one penny the first day, but your payment will double each day."

You mull it over. Initially, the first option seems like the much better bet. One million dollars, no drive, and no hassle. How could the second option be worth your while?

But then you do the math.

For twenty-six days, the second option seems like the losing proposition. At the end of the first week, you have collected a cumulative $0.64. On day 15—already halfway through the month—your boss hands over a paltry $163.84. But something incredible happens around day 26...

"Exponential" is one of *those* words. It tends to get tossed into conversation like a hyperbolic grenade. Like "sustainability", its meaning is hazy, its usage marked by hype and hysteria.

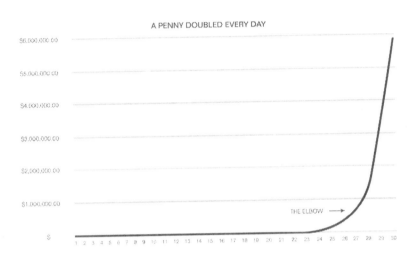

Diagram 1.1 | **A PENNY DOUBLED EVERY DAY**
A payment of one penny doubled every day of a thirty-day month sounds small, but the outcome would shock most organizations.

Perhaps what's most surprising about the concept of "the exponential"—and what gets overlooked or forgotten— is how extraordinarily simple it actually is. Exponential growth is achieved by a plain, old, steady, constant and compounding rate of growth or change. For example, the American Gross Domestic Product has grown by approximately 2% every year since World War II. Two percent: a predictable, long-established rate of growth that surprises no one. But over time, month by month, quarter by quarter, the impact of that yearly, compounding 2% gets steadily—and then dramatically—more significant.

If that growth is plotted on a graph, it appears as if very little is happening for a long time—growth is virtually flat, the line crawls along horizontally—then suddenly a miraculous "elbow" appears in the rate of growth, sending the line soaring upward. The line on our graph now resembles a hockey stick. In the context of the annual 2% compounded growth of American GDP, that hockey stick heralds the sudden arrival of a supreme world power on the global stage. The elbow in the hockey stick is the point at which exponential change reached a tipping point and blew up, sending American fortunes soaring.

The truth is that human beings have always lived with exponential change. Growth and development have always occurred at what appeared to be steady rates. Rates that, after a long period of time, kicked up at the end in a way that made change feel like it had just occurred. And, because a system of interconnected factors is always at play, it is never just a single change taking place. It took us 8,000 years to transition from the Agrarian Age to the Industrial Revolution, but only 120 years after that, we were manufacturing light bulbs. 90 years after that: the moon landing. 22 years after that: the Internet. 9 years after that: a sequenced human genome. The exponential factor has been with us for a long time.

When we take that bird's eye view of human history, it is dazzling, but how often do we do that? For the most part we are submerged in the minutiae of our daily lives, where the terrain is fairly predictable. Indeed, the reality of exponential change confounds our very brains, which are wired for learning that is predicated on a linear relationship between cause and effect. We expect almost instant feedback from an action. If there is any delay outside our immediate, expected timeframe then we tend to separate effect from cause. For millennia our experience has been that in most cases what was true yesterday will be true tomorrow. Our survival traditionally depended upon storing up information about the past in order to skilfully navigate the present and future.

The elbow of the exponential presents a very different environment. The magnitude of change increases so much in the elbow that it registers in the arena of daily life. At this point, what was true yesterday bears absolutely no resemblance to the potential reality of tomorrow. When this occurs, change truly feels *present*. It seems sudden, shocking, magical, unforseen, and confounding, like a phenomenon that "came out of nowhere." An overnight success—or failure.

Another way of understanding the elbow is as a threshold where the magnitude or intensity of a change in conditions passes the point of no return. Change shoots up through the elbow into a place that is removed from our sense of the present and the past. At this point, fighting change is futile. Going back and trying to recover the past to retain continuity is folly. In the eye of the exponential storm this simply wastes valuable resources.

This is disruption: the point at which exponential change can be felt at the level of daily life. It's the moment in time when you can no longer ignore change even if you wanted to. It's what occurs between Day 26 and Day 30, and it packs an unexpected punch.

HOW BIG A PUNCH? WELL, ON DAY 30, YOUR BOSS GAVE YOU YOUR LAST DAY'S PAY ACCORDING TO HIS EXPONENTIAL TERMS. ON THAT DAY, YOU RECEIVED $5,368,709.12. AND YOUR BOSS THANKS HEAVEN IT WASN'T A 31-DAY MONTH.

FEELING DISRUPTED?

We now live in a world in which obscure start-ups like YouTube, Facebook, and Airbnb each respectively secured a billion users (or a billion and a half in the case of Facebook) in a single decade. In that same decade, a "drone" went from being a military weapon system to being a toy that could be purchased for a child for $50.

Or consider the phenomenon of "the Internet of Everything" (IoE), in which experts are forecasting a 400% growth in Machine-to-Machine (M2M) connections over the next five years. By 2018 there's likely to be over 10 billion connected devices, and by 2020 some observers predict over 70 billion. Add Big Data to IoE, and it's tough to predict just how big the impact will be on the already complex culture of digital transactions.

Of course exponential change isn't just expressing itself through technology or commerce. Scientists touring the Russian Artic Ocean to check for plumes of noxious methane gas recently encountered a troubling phenomenon. Where they formerly found hundreds of meter-wide plumes, now there are hundreds of kilometer-wide columns of gas bubbling out of the ocean waters. Methane gas is fifty times more damaging to the atmosphere than carbon dioxide. Warming thaws Arctic sea ice, eroding the natural "mirror" that reflects heat back into space, which then raises the temperature of the ocean even higher, and so on. Nature, too, is a matrix of elbows, threshold breaches and tipping points that are accelerating changes—in this case changes to the climatic patterns that provide a stable platform for existence as we know it.

Will digital disruption pale into insignificance relative to the climate hockey stick? Or, will digital be the disruptive influence that, if leveraged in the right way, provides us with exponential solutions to exponential climate change?

The truth is that we are living in the "exponential elbow" of many different but interconnected sectors and systems. It's a pile-up of hockey sticks, a kind of global 26th day, when change is chronic and systemic. This is the age of disruption, in which the change that was always developing at an exponential rate suddenly and profoundly accelerates, reshaping the reality of everyday life. It's the moment when we wake-up, startled and disoriented, in a bed we've been sleeping in for millennia.

So how does it feel to be an individual living at a time when exponential change registers in the arena of everyday life? How do these "elbows" manifest in your personal experience, at work or in your home? From yesterday's rush of cloud computing, to the rapid changes in climate patterns, to a Big Data driven IoE, how is your everyday existence shifting?

PAUSE AND CONSIDER: *What does your disruption look like? What are your disruptors?*

THE FIVE FACTORS OF DISRUPTIVE CHANGE

If the theory of exponential change is a simple concept to understand, the reality of life in times of disruption is anything but. The lived experienced of disruptive change is awesomely disorienting and difficult to parse.

These "exponential elbows" can *feel* like magic, rather than mere math. But if the sum of all of these accelerating changes is so great in impact that it causes us to glaze over, blinking at the magnitude of it all without comprehension or a plan of attack, then perhaps it will serve us to break this disruptive era down in a little more detail.

In our work with organizations on the frontlines of disruption, you could say we've more or less gotten into the habit of reading signs of the times and making sense of them. That much scanning of the horizon does tend you give you a certain sense of perspective. So while we feel the miracle and the peril of living in this 26th day as keenly as anyone, we've found ways of breaking it down so that it makes more sense.

After two decades of working with organizations, we have identified five factors that are driving disruptive exponential change. They are connectivity, complexity, chaos and change cycles. At the intersection of these four factors is the fifth: technological development.

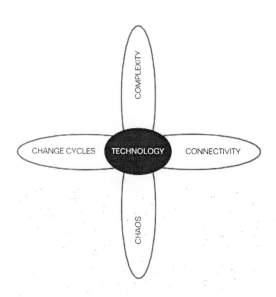

Diagram 1.2 | **THE FACTORS OF DISRUPTIVE CHANGE**
Five intrinsically linked factors that drive disruption.

It is important to note that these factors are intrinsically connected. Together, they create a matrix of systemic change where developments in one component cause a cascade of accelerated developments in all others. But for now, let's disconnect the dots by taking a closer look at each of the driving factors of exponential acceleration.

WELCOME TO YOUR WHISTLESTOP TOUR OF THE AGE OF DISRUPTIVE CHANGE.

Connectivity

Why did Facebook acquire a billion and a half users in a little more than a decade? Why have a plethora of social media businesses—from LinkedIn to SnapChat to Pinterest to Twitter to Instagram to Tumblr—exploded in influence and income over the same time period? eBay founder Pierre Omidyar alludes to it elegantly in the above quote. Human beings yearn to build networks. We are irrepressible connectors, the species that shares information in order to prosper. Social media merely represents an acceleration of a rather ancient human imperative.

> ❝ *WE HAVE TECHNOLOGY, FINALLY, THAT FOR THE FIRST TIME IN HUMAN HISTORY ALLOWS PEOPLE TO REALLY MAINTAIN RICH CONNECTIONS WITH MUCH LARGER NUMBERS OF PEOPLE.*❞
>
> *Pierre Omidyar*

While social media is certainly the most populist expression of the great connectivity shift, this trend is working its way through all systems of information, communication, education, production, and trade. The elimination of a time lag between communicators has cranked up the speed of network building while the elimination of geographic constraints has fostered connections, transactions, and collaborations that would have been inconceivable even twenty years ago. Just as the IoE grows, so too does the incidence of radical new economic models predicated on a culture of connectivity. For example, the rise of corporation-disrupting peer-to-peer businesses like Airbnb and Uber represents a whole new class of entrepreneurs waking up to the power of local and global connectivity.

Eduardo Paes once claimed that "economic integration was the first strong evidence of a new era" and it's hard to disagree with him. As the spaces between us narrow, the economic opportunities expand—as do the hazards of failure. Economic imperative and our irrepressible desire to connect have produced a momentum with which traditional governing bodies have a very difficult time keeping pace.

Globalization means open markets, stiffer competition, immense niche opportunities, and a world-sized market that sets the quality standards for all. It has brought us call centres staffed by immaculate English-speaking Filipinos and scandals over toxic dog treats from Chinese factories. It has created waves of fear in the "developed" world's labor market over the ramifications of outsourcing. But it is also creating hungry new markets for a variety of goods and services.

CONSIDER THE FOLLOWING:

- Emerging markets are currently projected to grow four times as fast as developed markets.

- About $20 trillion USD, or 35% of all consumer spending, will take place in emerging markets by 2020.

- 270 million new households from emerging markets will enter the "global consuming class" (ie. those to whom you want to be marketing) between 2010 and 2020. This represents an increase of more than 40%.

The Boston Consulting Group, whose Global Readiness Index assesses the ability of businesses to capture the growth, scale, and cost advantages of developing countries, recently conducted a survey that revealed only 13% of senior executives feel equipped to capitalize on these emerging opportunities. There is just as much hand wringing over increased opportunity as there is over increased competition, and risk.

But in today's connected world, leveraging connectivity shouldn't be seen as a difficult proposition. For the past ten years or so we've watched Apple and Amazon dominate product categories in global markets. We're now used to "Facebooking" and being "friended", "poked", "liked" and "tweeted" and if recent start-ups like Uber or Airbnb can do it, why can't others?

PAUSE AND CONSIDER: *How connected to your customers is your organization, and what networks do you "own" in the same manner as Facebook, Apple or Amazon?*

Complexity

Connectivity is a major driver of complexity. A dissection of any corporation's supply chain in the globalized

" *THE ART OF SIMPLICITY IS A PUZZLE OF COMPLEXITY.*"

Douglas Horton

era will drive home the reality of our highly complex milieu.

As newly connected parties find novel ways to combine their diverse capabilities, complexity in our society, economy, and technology deepens. It increases the density of the networked parties, the speed at which they transact, and the interdependencies that form between them.

What's interesting about complexity is that it finds a foothold in our thinking only to the degree that our understanding of it and our interactions with it can be made simple. As consumers, we want to engage with processes and products that do not challenge us too much intellectually or drain us emotionally. The smart device was an incredible leap forward in terms of complex technology. But, it took off among consumers because Apple leveraged complexity and created a simple interface that was delightfully intuitive.

Banks may be the ultimate example of complexity made to appear simple. Picture an ATM. It's an interface not much more complicated than a child's toy, available for convenient and quick transactions that actually represent an awesome choreography of commerce, law, security, and technology. All we need to do is push the buttons and take the cash. Simple.

Or consider the humble sandwich. How many pairs of hands does it take to make a sandwich? One? Not a chance. Your lunch is the end result of a veritable sandwich-making network spanning the globe. Farmers raised the wheat. Bakers made the bread. Truck drivers transported the condiments. The electric company powered the café that served it. The girl behind the counter may even have sprinkled it with some salt from Hervé Rocheteau on Île de Ré, a small island off the western coast of France. Your sandwich is a marvel of modern complexity made to appear simple.

PAUSE AND CONSIDER: *How does your organization take what is complex and make it appear simple?*

Chaos

For our purposes, chaos can be best explained as the amount of discontinuity in a system or network. Such a system could be an organization, an economy, a society or a climate. Discontinuity is simply anything that breaks from the norm, or the continuity we are used to. It's when known variables can no longer be relied on to predict an outcome. This can be experienced as an unexpected extreme weather event, a disease that has never previously been identified, or a global financial crisis that most people don't see coming.

> " *THE BATTLEFIELD IS A SCENE OF CONSTANT CHAOS. THE WINNER WILL BE THE ONE WHO CONTROLS THAT CHAOS, BOTH HIS OWN AND THE ENEMY'S."*
>
> *Napoleon Bonaparte*

In 1942, the economist Joseph Schumpeter published *Capitalism, Socialism, and Democracy*, his treatise on economic innovation. In it, he wrote:

> *The process of creative destruction is the essential fact about capitalism...The new commodity, the new technology, the new source of supply, the new type of organization...which strikes not at the margins of the profits and the outputs of the existing firms but at their foundations and their very lives.*

Schumpeter's term for the "process of industrial mutation that incessantly revolutionizes the economic structure from within" was "creative destruction". You could also use terms like disruption or discontinuity. We prefer the word "chaos", because it pulls no punches.

In many instances, chaos in today's world is human-made. Just think of all the discontinuous technologies throughout human history that set the scene for the old ways of doing things to become redundant. In some ways man's lust for creative expression can mean the self-sown seeds of discontinuity and chaos.

Nowadays, chaos proliferates in all sectors. It can strike certain ventures dead and raise new opportunities in their place. As chaos ramps up, the shelf life of any innovation will shrink. So too will our ability to hang on to cash cows for any length of time. The frenetic pace of social media platform creation and obsolescence is only one indicator of chaos. Remember MySpace?

In chaos, change is the only constant. There are two varieties of change: continuous and discontinuous. Continuous change is precedented or predictable change, like the familiar, orderly progression of winter into spring. Discontinuous change is the unexpected: a hurricane instead of springtime showers. Discontinuity is the rise of digital abruptly transforming Kodak's empire into a morass of stranded assets.

In chaos, one person's discontinuity can be another's continuity. Under Steve Jobs, Apple was primed for discontinuity. Not only did Apple perfect the smart device technology, but they also created an entirely new ecosystem of profit generation around it with iTunes and the App Store. For Apple, the digital hurricane wasn't a disaster. In fact, the hurricane was the creative destruction *they* caused as they leveraged discontinuity.

Leveraging chaos and discontinuity is an age-old tradition. Newton's mechanistic view of the world was a prime contributor to the machine-age of the Industrial Revolution, which was eventually overturned by Einstein's theory of relativity, which paved the way for nuclear power, the space race, and GPS. Disruption, chaos, discontinuity, creative destruction... it's all old hat, really. As with all factors driving exponential change, chaos has always been with us, it's just that its impact is ratcheting up.

Chaos may not be comfortable, but leveraging discontinuity is a survival skill in the age of disruption. And unfortunately, it's an uncommon skill. Too often, we are driven by cognitive biases such as Fixed Action Patterns (or FAPs) that blind us to the reality of our situation and prevent us from taking positive action. When working with organizations we've noticed that "FAPs" are just one example of the cognitive biases that can blind people to inevitable, disruptive change. Here are some more:

AMBIGUITY EFFECT - The tendency to avoid options for which missing information makes the outcome seem "unknown".

AVAILABILITY CASCADE - A self-reinforcing process in which a collective belief gains more and more plausibility through its increasing repetition in public discourse (otherwise known as "repeat something long enough and it will become true").

BANDWAGON EFFECT - The tendency to do (or believe) things because many other people do (or believe) the same (also known as "groupthink").

CONFIRMATION BIAS - The tendency to search for, interpret, focus on and remember information in a way that confirms one's preconceptions.

ILLUSION OF CONTROL – The tendency to overestimate one's ability to control events.

NEGLECT OF PROBABILITY - The tendency to completely disregard probability when making a decision under uncertainty.

PAUSE AND CONSIDER: *Can you think of other biases that emerge when people you know are confronted with chaos? Do you fall prey to any of these biases? Or, do you face discontinuity head-on?*

Change Cycles

When we examine connectivity, complexity, and chaos more closely, it becomes increasingly clear that these are horses running in tandem, pulling a common chariot. And this chariot runs on wheels that keep turning more and more quickly.

When we talk about change cycles, we refer to the time it takes for a cycle of change to be complete. For example: the time it takes to learn and apply something, to produce something, to complete a transaction, for an invention to become the norm, or for a start-up to become a force to be reckoned

" IN 2009, AT THE HEIGHT OF THE GLOBAL ECONOMIC CRISIS, IT WAS CLEAR THAT WE WERE SEEING SOMETHING NEW: THE IMPACTS OF THE CRISIS WERE FLOWING ACROSS BORDERS AT UNPRECEDENTED VELOCITY."

Ban Ki-moon

with. To get a sense of how change cycles are speeding up just think about how long it once took to order and receive a hamburger. In the 1940s people were prepared to wait around for twenty minutes. Now, if it's not in your hands within three, the fast food outlet is toast. Then there's Uber's growth from a simple app to a $50 billion business in six years and Pinterest's movement from 40,000 users in 2010 to 70 million by the end of 2013. All of these developments represent accelerating change cycles.

Obviously, the change cycle takes on a dizzying array of faces. It has been called the stock cycle, the business cycle, the transaction cycle, and on and on. And it is difficult to look anywhere and find instances where change cycles are not beginning to operate at hyper-speeds.

We behold accelerating change cycles when we see a news-making event trending on Twitter mere minutes after it first occurred. We participate in accelerating change cycles when we click a button to conduct a financial transaction that would have required six months of formal letter writing a century ago. We keenly feel our vulnerability within accelerated change cycles when new start-ups producing more relevant technologies make the old-guard companies we banked our future on suddenly obsolete. Occasionally, these rapidly revolving wheels raise so much dust that it becomes difficult to perceive whether one, in fact, has any future to bank on at all. At best, seeing further than the end of your nose becomes a challenge. At worst, we wonder if the horses carrying this inexorable chariot forward might not have an apocalyptic lineage.

As overwhelming as any one of these sped-up change cycles might be, the incredible fact is each one has the tendency to multiply the acceleration of other change cycles. This, above all else, is how you need to think about the era of disruption: a rapid convergence of multiple, systemic change cycles that continually trigger one another to create a compounded effect of system-wide and ever-accelerating exponential change.

PAUSE AND CONSIDER: *Which accelerating change cycles are impacting your organization?*

Technology: The Paradox at The Intersection

In 1965, Intel co-founder Gordon Moore observed that the number of transistors per square inch on integrated circuits had doubled every year since the invention of the integrated circuit. He figured the trend would continue indefinitely and for a while his prediction was spot-on. After a number of years, the pace slowed down to the point where data density doubled every 18 months

" OUR INTUITION ABOUT THE FUTURE IS LINEAR. BUT THE REALITY OF INFORMATION TECHNOLOGY IS EXPONENTIAL, AND THAT MAKES A PROFOUND DIFFERENCE. IF I TAKE 30 STEPS LINEARLY, I GET TO 30. IF I TAKE 30 STEPS EXPONENTIALLY, I GET TO A BILLION."

Ray Kurzweil

and since then, the trend has been holding steady. As we move on from conventional chip technology, no one can predict with any authority when "Moore's Law" might cease to hold true. There are some, like the famed futurist Kurzweil, who don't believe it ever will. In 2001, he wrote that: "We won't experience 100 years of progress in the

21st century — it will be more like 20,000 years of progress (at today's rate)."

This is where the *Wired* enthusiast in you is likely to get worked up. This is where the parable of the daily-doubling pennies becomes truly pertinent. While big-thinking futurists like Kurzweil have their share of detractors, it remains true that we are currently living in a world predicted by Moore's law, and where evidence of the exponential pace of technological development is easy to find. And when we find it, it unsettles us at least as often as it inspires us.

When American political activist Cody Wilson test-fired the world's first 3-D printed handgun in May 2013, it truly was a shot heard around the world. The pistol, dubbed the Liberator, had reportedly been printed out of $60 USD worth of plastic with a Stratasys Dimension series 3D printer that Wilson bought on eBay. After firing the gun, Wilson published its blueprints through Defense Distributed, a non-profit that Wilson established to publicize open-source gun designs or "wiki weapons."

Wilson's feat alarmed law enforcement officials, attracted massive media attention, and sparked widespread debate over how to meaningfully regulate the activities that this radical new technology suddenly seemed capable of facilitating. Wilson's gun was aptly named the Liberator, even if all he intended was to evoke his crypto-anarchist ideology, rather than the stunning horizon of possibility opened up by the disruptive power of technology.

Technological development sits at the intersection of these five synergistic drivers of exponential change. If you like, it is the actual energy driving connectivity, complexity, and chaos. Technology is behind change cycles speeding up at an ever-increasing rate. It is the vehicle that carries us rapidly into the exponential future.

Herein lies the paradox of technology. It hurtles us forward into unprecedented experiences, but at the same time it facilitates a smooth ride. It is the tool that helps us to make sense of and derive benefit from our radically changing world. It is the ATM or the smart device that represents the delivery of incomprehensibly complex forces in simple, user-friendly packages.

As with all factors of exponential change, we've been passengers on the technological ride since we first walked the earth. When we first harnessed fire and built tools from stone, we set the wheels of disruption in motion. From fire, to the wheel, to the Gutenberg press, to the stream driven machine, to the smart device, it's been one long, wild ride that speeds up as it travels further. And once again, it's the acceleration that's hard to cope with. When Boston Consulting reports that only 13% of senior executives feel equipped to pursue global opportunities it means that 87% are having trouble.

And generating value is the name of the game. Our technologies have little merit unless they enhance our capability to generate sustainable value. Technology is valuable when it helps us keep pace with change, despite the complexity, chaos, unpredictability, or velocity of our challenges.

So shouldn't we use our capability for developing new technology to create decision-making processes that will work the same way? Surely we need strategic tools that will help us to navigate these staggering challenges as simply and logically as possible. We need tools of the mind that will allow us to keep up with these accelerating change cycles. "Going lean" isn't the answer. Pursuing agile management or flex-organization half-heartedly isn't the answer. Something entirely more radical is in order.

We need an approach designed specifically for disruptive environments. We need a harness that leverages the energy, tension and speed of the horses pulling the chariot of disruption. If we are to see ourselves as charioteers rather than unlucky souls ground under the wheels, we need to grab hold of the right philosophy *quickly*.

THAT'S WHAT WE MUST NOW EXPLORE.

First, A Word About Resilience

Much of our work focuses on making organizations more resilient in the face of disruptive change, but whenever we use the world "resilience", we are aware of what that word signifies for most people. It makes sense to pause for a moment and clarify what it means to us and why we hope

" I HAVE NOTICED EVEN PEOPLE WHO CLAIM EVERYTHING IS PREDESTINED, AND THAT WE CAN DO NOTHING TO CHANGE IT, LOOK BEFORE THEY CROSS THE ROAD."

Stephen Hawking

to instil a new form of resilience in organizations using Strategy in Action (SiA) as they learn to navigate the elbows of exponential change.

In our culture, resilience is normally understood to be the quality possessed by a survivor, one who lives and breathes and succeeds despite all calamities, shocks and adversities. So far, we're on board. But usually, we see the survivor-resilience trajectory play out like this: survivor motors along, unaware of the troubles to come; survivor runs smack into adversity; survivor is hurt, compromised, and laid low; and finally, survivor stands up, shakes off the dust, and marches on, resuming his or her original course. Fall down and get back up. Take a licking and keep on ticking.

What we notice is that this type of survival veers precipitously close to the experience of victimization. In this popular resilience narrative, you don't know if the hero will be a victim or a survivor until the final frame.

Now, obviously, there's no way to do business or live one's life without drawing upon this type of resilience from time to time. We would never suggest that all adversity can be avoided. But sometimes, when we hear this resilience narrative repeated time and time again, we can't help but wonder, "Couldn't there have been another way?"

In our view, there's a type of resilience that is often overlooked, a resilience that we haven't built up quite as many myths around. In our version of the resilience narrative the survivor looks ahead, figuring out how to alter his or her course before disruptive change becomes adversity. In our version of the story, the survivor experiences the change positively and doesn't spend any time laid low. In our version of the story, the victim doesn't become the survivor in the final frame—the adversity becomes the opportunity and the final frame is re-written.

When we talk about resilience, we do not mean to talk about weathering shocks, surviving a crisis, or remaining securely buckled into a smashed-up vehicle like a Crash

Test Dummy. We are talking about learning how to *change ahead of change.*

How do you change ahead of change? It's spelled out in the alternative story of resilience. First, you do it by changing the way you see the world. By changing the way you see "adversity" or disruptive change. Like the 13% of executives who are throwing themselves eagerly into figuring out how to capitalize on those burgeoning emerging markets, this version of resilience comes through embracing discontinuous, disruptive change and learning how to flow with it and ride on top of it. How will the remaining 87% experience the tremendous changes globalization is bringing? Without this new kind of resilience they will likely experience it as a crushing wave of competitive disadvantage. When an opportunity on the horizon is ignored it often arrives in the form of adversity. Remember Kodak.

So, for us, it's all about resilience. But keep in mind that we're talking about bouncing back only if you need to, and not as the only available course of action. We're more interested in reframing resilience and talking about changing the capability of your organization. Its time to tune-in to this disruptive era so that you can experience these changes as incoming opportunities instead of continually crashing up against them like hapless Crash Test Dummies.

THE BOTTOM LINE IS THIS: IF CHANGES ARE COMING OUR WAY AT AN EXPONENTIAL RATE, HOW CAN WE EXPERIENCE THEM AS OPPORTUNITIES RATHER THAN ADVERSITIES? BEFORE WE DIVE INTO THE SIA ALGORITHM IN CHAPTER 2, LET'S LAY SOME GROUNDWORK BY UNPACKING HOW WE THINK ABOUT CHANGE, RESILIENCE, RISK, AND OPPORTUNITY.

A Checklist for Crash Test Dummy Syndrome

We know that the disruptions beginning to cascade throughout all sectors of human experience will make the Industrial Revolution look like child's play. And it's ok for you and your organization to feel uncomfortable in the face of so much change coming at you at an accelerating rate.

> " SINCE WE CANNOT CHANGE REALITY, LET US CHANGE THE EYES WHICH SEE REALITY."
>
> Nikos Kazantzakis

Change is hard. It's beyond a cliché. We prefer the predictable and continuous because we are all creatures who like to build on prior successes, honoring precedent and tradition. We can all dance, but we are often more comfortable when the steps are choreographed.

We're so wired to resist change that we often mistake chaos and creative destruction for crisis. We may even be convinced that change is a force wholly devoted to the destruction of life, and miss the promise of revitalizing opportunity that is always embedded within it.

We have compiled a list of typical responses to disruptive change. Read through it and take an opportunity to do a self-check. Which items ring a bell for you? When sudden overwhelming changes loom, threatening to knock you off of your course, what is your most likely response?

Do you...

Miss it completely?

"We had no idea the sub prime crisis was coming down the pipeline! How could we have known? No one could have reasonably foreseen these circumstances!"

Deny that it is happening?

"We just didn't want to believe digital was the ascendant technology."

Beat a dead horse?

"We've *always* raised good money with our direct mailing list. We need to write better appeals and send more of them. We just have to work harder, that's all!"

Try to actively arrest or reverse the trend?

"If we just keep Steve Sassons's filmless camera in the closet, we'll kill the technology and maintain the Kodak cash cow."

Take the hit and do your best to 'bounce back'?

"Yes, the North American car manufacturing industry is little laid-low at the moment, but if you just write us a check, I'm sure we'll bounce back. After all, we get credit for just *surviving*, don't we?"

Act like the space cadet floating above it all, seeing everything in only the most hyper-positive terms?

"If we simply recycle our cans and newspapers, everything's going to be just fine! If not, life on Mars is an alternative."

...or only in the most hyper-negative light?

"The end is nigh! If we don't immediately convert our motor vehicles into garden planters, we'll all be dead in a half-century!"

These are the sentiments of people and organizations afflicted by Crash Test Dummy Syndrome. Hurtling along at high speed towards a wall, they appear inanimate and helpless, but securely strapped in for what promises to be a most bumpy ride. For these ones, resilience means the ability to bounce-back, because they can't be held accountable for being hit hard in the first place. The best they can aspire to is survival.

BUT WHAT IF THOSE POOR HAPLESS DUMMIES COULD LIBERATE THEMSELVES FROM THEIR CRASH-AND-SURVIVE CYCLE BY THINKING ABOUT CHANGE DIFFERENTLY?

Grow and Conserve—But Not Without Releasing and Re-Organizing

In many ways, the ecologist Buzz Holling has revolutionized the concept of change simply by being a good observer. His contributions to industries and schools of thought as diverse as change management and the sustainability movement are based on noticing how nature appears to actually work—as opposed to the way we assume it should.

" EVERY CORNY THING THAT'S SAID ABOUT LIVING WITH NATURE - BEING IN HARMONY WITH THE EARTH, FEELING THE CYCLE OF THE SEASONS - HAPPENS TO BE TRUE."

Susan Orlean

Traditionally, ecologists believed that ecologies worked like this: plants take over an area (growth) and then they work for their own survival by slowly accumulating energy from and within the surrounding environment (conversation). So, for example, a tree grows, storing up energy from the sun and rain and nutrients in the soil, and it conserves all of that energy in its leaf and wood-mass and root system. This tree is an entity set to grow and survive. Growth and conservation.

But Holling saw two other equally important forces at play in thriving ecologies: release and reorganization. When ecologies like forests develop, certain species (eg. large hardwood trees) become dominant. But the energy that these dominant species accumulate also represents the potential for new ecologies, new species, and new kinds of environments. All of that accumulated energy is always ready to be released into startlingly new forms of life. For example, occasionally the energy in the wood becomes fuel for a wildfire that transforms the landscape, making it more hospitable to different kinds of plants. If you like, this is nature's version of creative destruction.

Holling's "adaptive cycle" envisions change moving in two directions: a forward loop of growth and conservation, and a backward loop of release and reorganization— helping us to understand when to reap rewards, and when to foster destruction and innovation. Some of the energy of a thriving ecology will always be directed towards breaking down the system to create something else completely new. This backward loop doesn't result in disaster because these episodes of breaking-down-to-build-back-up are nested within larger patterns of stability and forward looping. If one part of the forest succumbs to a landscape-transforming wildfire, there is still plenty of hardwood forest in the world that keeps growing and storing up energy in the form of towering foliage, wood-mass and mighty root systems.

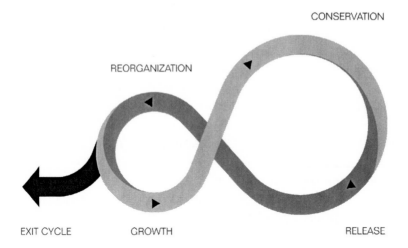

CONSERVATION

REORGANIZATION

EXIT CYCLE   GROWTH   RELEASE

Diagram 1.3 | **THE ADAPTIVE CYCLE**

Holling's "Adaptive Cycle" with its forward loop of growth and conservation, and backward loop of release and reorganization. Failing to understand this thinking may cause an exit to a cycle of M.A.D (Managed Adaptive Decline).

As usual, we can learn a thing or two from nature. In the bigger picture, ecologies thrive because of "disastrous episodes" that lead to novel outcomes, not in spite of them. A wildfire is part of the natural cycle, not an aberration within it. Disruptive or "destructive" change, therefore, is just accumulated energy being expressed in novel ways. It's never, as we like to say, "the end of the world". It is, in fact, the way of the world, and ever has it been.

Holling's adaptive cycle applies equally to social and economic systems. The Roman Empire and many empires that followed fell into the trap of holding on too long to the benefits of colonization and ultimately became victims of their own greed. The huge business empires of the past have also succumbed to similar fates by thinking they could lock-in and control markets and customers through strangling competitive innovation. Just think about old-school media outlets, vehicle manufacturers and (more recently) energy companies.

When leaders insist on celebrating the forward-loop and fearing, denying, or attempting to obstruct the backward loop, they are choosing to be out of step with nature itself. Efficiency and conservation are only one side of the adaptive cycle within which all systems operate. Equally important are the backward looping forces of innovation, wherein stored-up energy is released to create something new, a fundamental re-organization of the system.

You can't grow a company to a massive size and simply conserve its wealth and maintain its structure. Some of the accumulated energy of that wealth is always going to veer off into self-induced creative destruction or be hit by unforeseen discontinuity, whether you like it or not. Kodak's Steve Sasson and his ilk are always going to be puttering around in unsupervised laboratories, setting wildfires where their managers would prefer them to just straighten up and grow tall, like well-behaved hardwoods. Leaders are faced with a choice. They can either honor the backward loop of change, seeing it as a force for revitalization, or attempt to fight it, and inevitably experience it as a world-destroying conflagration.

Grow your organization. Tend to it so that it operates as an efficient entity that accumulates and conserves energy in the form of capability, capital, intellectual property, human resources, everything else that constitutes a thriving operation. But release some of that energy into leveraging discontinuity, even if doing so appears to threaten "business as usual", undermining the very structure that has historically secured success for you. Realize that that this "release" contains the seeds of re-organization that will allow you to endure.

Organizations like Kodak, who chose to stick doggedly to "growing and conserving" without "releasing and reorganizing", have fallen into Managed Adaptive Decline. They blindly adapt to unfavorable conditions in a well-managed manner that initially appears to mitigate disruption but quickly accelerates destructive decline. M.A.D. organizations know what worked in the past, and they're damned if they're going to change course just because the world is changing around them. The answer for these folks is always to just work harder and become more efficient at carrying out business as usual. When they discuss change, they are quick to fall into cognitive bias or utter the justifications and lamentations we included in our Crash Test Dummy Checklist.

IN A VERY REAL WAY, THEY HAVE CHOSEN TO SET THEMSELVES AGAINST NATURE. COULD THERE POSSIBLY BE A BETTER DEFINITION OF MADNESS?

A CHECKLIST FOR DISRUPTIVE LEADERSHIP

Yes, it *is* possible to make peace with change—even disruptive change. It begins with thinking about change differently, and seeing it as a natural process of release and reorganization. But resilience is more than an attitude or a philosophy. There are practical markers of living in tune with an age of exponentially accelerating change.

The following is a checklist for an organization or a leader that is free of the dreaded Crash Test Dummy Syndrome. This organization will not succumb to the deceptively respectable stance of MAD. Run through this list and see for yourself how you stack up.

Are you...

Tuned in to change?

Do you pay attention to what's happening in your world? Do you understand what forces are shaping your reality today and which ones are rolling over the horizon?

Embracing complexity?

Do you understand how to embrace complexity and offer solutions that appear simple and that people will value? Do you think of new ways for diverse parties to come together to create novel processes, products, or experiences? Do you think about how a variety of capabilities can be leveraged? Are you excited by the possibilities?

Leveraging discontinuity and chaos?

Are you a Kodak or an Apple? Do you see disruptions as opportunities to be the first one in line to create something valuable? Are you aware that holding onto stranded assets is a one-way ticket to failure?

Connected to networks?

Do you see yourself or your organization as a node in a

web of relationships? Do you look for ways to build those relationships or connections? Do you actively leverage the power of networks both on and offline?

Tech-savvy?

Do you keep up with technological developments so that you can figure out which new tools are going to help you do what you do better or differently? Do you use technology to make your life simpler, rather than more complicated?

Changing ahead of change?

Are you resilient through changing ahead of change, or do you constantly fall prey to bouncing back and pushing through adversity – like a typical Crash Test Dummy? Do you release and re-organize? Do you prepare yourself to ride the wave rather than flounder in its wake?

THE CONFIDENT PENNY COLLECTOR

The idea that we are living during a time when "exponential elbows" are piling up into a vast matrix of accelerating changes cannot help but rattle us. It's only natural. We feel the anxiety whether we're actively paying attention or not. These changes are so profound and pervasive that we can't help but register them. Those 87% of executives who aren't planning for globalization's explosion of new markets still know that something's up, and they aren't necessarily feeling good about it. Unlike you, they may end up choosing option number one, the million-dollar payday that leaves them in the dust.

But there is a better way. Disruptive times call for a philosophy of change that instills true resilience – to change ahead of change rather than bouncing back from shocks or constantly pushing through adversity. Managed Adaptive Decline and Crash Test Dummy Syndrome are not options for true leaders in an age of disruptive change. True leaders will leverage the exponential, turn their pennies into dollars and collect their $5 million at the end of the month as the elbow sends them soaring upwards.

CONFIDENCE IS POSSIBLE. AND IT'S NECESSARY ON THE 26TH DAY.

CHAPTER 2

Thinking Strategy in Action

AN ALGORITHM FOR STRATEGY AT THE SPEED OF DISRUPTION

AN INTRODUCTION TO STRATEGY IN ACTION (SIA), AN ALGORITHM THAT TEACHES US TO USE NATURALLY OCCURRING COGNITIVE TOOLS TO STRATEGIZE IN A COMPLEX, CHAOTIC AND FAST-MOVING REALITY.

" *AN EXPERT IS SOMEONE WHO HAS SUCCEEDED IN MAKING DECISIONS AND JUDGMENTS SIMPLER THROUGH KNOWING WHAT TO PAY ATTENTION TO AND WHAT TO IGNORE.*"

EDWARD DE BONO

FIVE PRECEPTS FOR ENJOYING THE RIDE

Near the beginning of Russell Banks' 2008 novel *The Reserve*, the Hemingwayesque Jordan Groves takes his love interest Vanessa Cole for a ride in his airplane over the Adirondack wilderness. Now, we all know that adrenaline heightens romantic sensibility, so when the altimeter reads 2,250 feet, Jordan invites Vanessa to take over. She takes control of the plane and Jordan starts her first flying lesson.

"You're sure you've never flown an airplane?"

"Never!"

He said, "Ok. Five things to remember! Five precepts."

She laughed. "Only five?"

"*Observe! Think! Plan! Execute!* And *abandon*! You use *abandon* if *execute* doesn't work, and then you go back to *observe*!"

"Okay!" she shouted. "You're crazy, you know!"

How crazy *is* Jordan? And how quick a student of the Five-Precept Flight Plan is Vanessa, who had been strolling along the lakefront as an attractive complement to the scenery mere hours earlier?

Jordan tells Vanessa to start by *observing* the altitude, bearing, and speed of the biplane. Next, she *observes* the "the moonlit roof of the clubhouse and some other smaller buildings nearby and the broad expanse of the golf course and then more dark forest and beyond the forest the mountains, Sentinel and the big one, Goliath." *Mountains.* Time for precept number two. Vanessa *thinks* and realizes they are not high enough. She then *plans*, deciding to give the biplane more power in order to increase their altitude. Vanessa's *execution*, however, lacks sufficient speed and lift to avoid Goliath. Jordan knows she has to *abandon* the plan and cut hard to starboard. Vanessa turns the plane at the last second, when her only flight path is through a notch in a stand of pine trees. Jordan points at the notch, ordering her to *observe*.

They make it through the pine trees alive. Jordan, seasoned in his five precepts, takes the control yoke back.

INTRODUCING STRATEGY IN ACTION (SIA)

We know that we are living in the age of disruption, when exponential changes have begun to impact us in ways we can no longer ignore even as

> **" IF YOU HAVE A SENSE OF WHAT WORKS NATURALLY, IT'S HARD TO FAIL."**
> *Buckminster Fuller*

we struggle to understand them. Like Vanessa, we haven't been trained to do this. But the plane is moving quickly, the stakes are life-and-death high, and like it or not, we are holding the control yoke.

In this scenario, we need a whittled-down approach to flying an airplane. We need something like Jordan's crazy flight plan. His five precepts are a deceptively simple sequence that works even in the moments when the flight isn't working out. It's a logical cycle with built-in capacity for correction. It's an algorithm fit for a Hemingwayesque hero in high-adrenaline scenarios.

If Jordan's crazy, so are we.

Resilient Futures has spent the last two decades working with businesses, government organizations, and municipalities. As we all know, the last ten years have brought the first really forceful expressions of disruption to organizations and their planning methods. During that time, we've met people coping in a variety of ways.

We've encountered fearful and demotivated people. We've encountered teams bent on "going lean" to save whatever profit margin remains. We've encountered leaders who glaze over at the idea of strategy and cringe when confronted with change outside the norm. We've encountered confusion, denial, and resistance. We've also encountered brilliant people whose breakthroughs have fed into our signature approach to strategic thinking.

All of those experiences have helped us shape a unique strategic framework that, like Jordan's flight plan, comes in five easy pieces. It's a framework for strategic thinking that is algorithmic in its ability to mirror our intuitive behaviors.

This algorithm is Strategy in Action, or SiA for short. SiA consists of five steps that we outline in a logical sequence. The steps can flow rapidly together in a cycle that corrects itself when your course seems to have you headed toward a collision with disruption.

SiA may be applied at a rapid-fire rate in what we call micro cycle time. Or it may be applied over a longer cycle of time—weeks or months—or whatever is required to deal with the complexity and speed of the conditions that have been identified. It has been applied to projects, strategic plans, innovation strategies, and programs to transform entire organizations. It has even been used for personal career planning.

It's our experience that anyone can use SiA. Especially when the alternative is slamming into a granite slab.

Picture a football team. They begin acquiring a skill when their coach breaks down each detail of a maneuver for them. Then, they move through the sequence repeatedly during drills. It's an intentional, meticulous process. Ultimately, by the time they are out on the field, it's all muscle memory. In fact, when they are playing, they naturally make adjustments in the way they are executing learned skills in order to achieve their ultimate goal: winning the game. Nobody would deny that multiple, complex, and dynamic changes are occurring quickly during a typical football game, but skilled players are able to navigate these developments quite fluidly. They even manage to enjoy themselves.

SiA works in exactly the same way. Once you internalize the principles and master the skills, you are able to enter the field confidently. You see complex developments play out and feel clear about what they mean. You make natural and effective adjustments. You feel well-deserved pride when your team lands a victory.

SiA is an algorithm that is already wired in your mind and manifests as a set of natural, everyday cognitive tools. You already use these tools on a daily basis and may not even realize it. You have a natural tendency to observe conditions, strategize, act, and adapt as conditions shift. If you throw a barbeque for friends, you observe the weather, and then put up a tent if the sun is blazing too brightly or if rain clouds are threatening to open up over your dinner guests. When you walk your dog up to the crosswalk, you look both ways, and press the button that will eventually halt traffic. You let the leash go slack or hold it tautly based on the arrival of other dog walkers on the scene and the signals your own dog is giving you.

PAUSE AND CONSIDER: *Can you think of another everyday example of SiA-style strategizing?*

Whether you know it or not, you are an incredibly agile strategist. You understand conditions, you gauge the opportunities and risks, and you are always seeking to generate value through using capabilities, and doing so in short, sharp, iterative catalytic actions.

What you may not do quite as naturally is scale up these cognitive tools for use in more complex, abstract circumstances—particularly at a team, department, or organisational level. We find that people with stronger inborn strategic instincts do exactly this, even if they aren't completely aware of it. When they are grappling with complex, fast-moving situations such as the ones any organization is working its way through on a daily basis, these natural-born strategists instinctively run through the SiA algorithm. They naturally *think* SiA.

For those of us who have lost touch with our strategic instincts, thinking SiA in the context of fast-moving, complex, and abstract scenarios is possible, but it must be surfaced and learned systematically. It must be practiced until it is internalized and becomes a natural way of thinking. Then, through scaling its application within teams and departments, it can be institutionalized across an organization.

That's why we created *our* algorithm. To help people learn to think SiA, which is to say, apply their naturally occurring cognitive tools to more abstract and complex circumstances. Circumstances like aligning a team towards the pursuit of strategic goals in a milieu of exponentially accelerating change. SiA is for strategy at any scale, for any outcome.

SIA'S FIVE PRECEPTS: STRATEGY AT THE SPEED OF CHANGE

If Jordan's flight plan was designed to keep an aircraft from crashing, our algorithm is designed to help teams and leaders *leverage disruptive change to generate sustainable value.*

Remember that. That's the whole point. SiA helps leaders to treat circumstances of exponentially accelerating change as opportunities, because otherwise, these same circumstances will manifest as value-destroying crises.

In Chapters 3-7 we will unpack each of these precepts in greater detail, but for now, here's a quick overview. In brief, SiA entails:

- Reading, understanding and continually monitoring immediate and emergent **conditions**;

- Perceiving the **strategic opportunity-risks** (SORs) that those conditions reveal;

- Identifying the **sustainable value** you and your team can generate out of those SORs;

- Determining the **capabilities** that allow you and your organization to generate the sustainable value available within those SORs;

- Developing **catalytic actions** that build and launch the capabilities driving sustainable value generation.

Finally, you course-correct by returning to the beginning of the algorithm. Read conditions, figure out what they are telling you, and then adapt your strategy (in action) accordingly.

THE SIA WHEEL REVOLVES CONSTANTLY AND IN REAL-TIME.

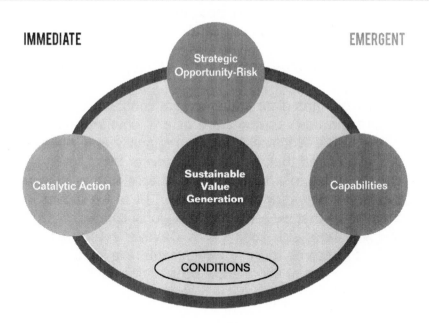

Diagram 2.1 | **THE SIA ALGORITHM**
The five precepts of Strategy in Action – Conditions, Strategic Opportunity-risk, Sustainable Value Generation, Capabilities and Catalytic Action.

The SiA vocabulary is a product of working with teams and leaders in the many realms of organizational strategy and change. Though the vocabulary may sound strange at times, they are everyday words taken straight from the dictionary. The words we use mean what they sound like they mean. For instance, listen to the weather report and you will hear talk about *conditions*. You know what they mean, right? *Opportunity* is exactly what it sounds like, and so is *risk*. We might combine these two to reinforce that you can never have an opportunity without risk (and vice versa) and call them opportunity-risks—but they're still just opportunities and risks. The same is true for *value* and *capability*. In SiA we use these words just as you use them. Finally, we use *catalytic* and *action* together to describe relatively small and rapid steps that combine to become catalytic in their energy and efficient in their synergy.

First Step: Read the Immediate and Emergent Conditions

We assess immediate and emergent conditions. We take an organization's temperature as it is now and may be in the future—internally, locally, regionally and globally. We understand that we are within one of these revolving change cycles in a vast network of accelerating change cycles. We understand— like those 13% of executives in Chapter 1—that we are actors in a global context. We are building those rich connections Omidyar referred to in order to become more knowledgeable. We keep an eye on the horizon of exponential possibilities—both positive and negative.

Second Step: Perceive Strategic Opportunity-Risks

As we look into conditions, we perceive the strategic opportunities and strategic risks that are inherent within those conditions. We see them combined as strategic opportunity-risks (or SORs). We imagine what value we might generate out of those SORs and we choose the ones we will actively pursue. We know that any disruptions on the horizon could represent our next big value-generating opportunity as long as we wisely manage the risk side of each SOR.

Third Step: Identify Value

We look more closely at the SORs that surround us in order to figure out which ones represent opportunities to generate the kind of value that is most important to us. This value must be sustainable, and produce benefits within and outside of our organization. The enduring value we generate is our best bet for resilience in the disruptive age.

Fourth Step: Determine Capabilities

We are now getting ready to act. We understand exactly how we might capitalize on those opportunities and manage those risks in order to generate sustainable value. We start seeing ourselves differently in light of those emergent opportunity-risks. We understand how we might need to change ahead of change. We figure out which capabilities we need to develop or acquire in order to generate sustainable value

Fifth Step: Develop Catalytic Actions

We design catalytic actions to build and execute the capabilities we need if we are going to generate value out of our SORs. We optimise our strengths and build the necessary networks. We prepare ourselves to benefit tremendously from the wall of power headed our way. We initiate synergistic systems of capability that make best use of our capabilities so that we are ready for the ride of our lives, rather than the destruction of everything we have built.

In reality—in *action*—these steps are bounded together in a cycle that never stops turning. When you are in your chosen aircraft, you never stop validating your course by checking conditions. There isn't really a single moment when you can stop paying attention to both the gauges inside of your aircraft and the terrain underneath or occasionally in front of you. SiA only works when you keep each of its precepts in continual alignment.

So how will you know when you fall out of alignment?

You'll know when you start feeling disoriented. The value you are seeking to generate will be eroding. Your capabilities will be out of sync with the situation at hand. The action you take will not have the desired effect. You will be hit by discontinuities and shocks from conditions you didn't see coming. Your people will experience the Crash Test Dummy Syndrome. Your organization may even start to go M.A.D.

PAUSE AND CONSIDER: *When was the last time your organization experienced symptoms like these? Can you now connect them to a problem with the way your team strategizes?*

To remain oriented, SiA's five precepts must be aligned and working in sync. This is why we follow the First Principle of SiA:

TO GENERATE SUSTAINABLE VALUE, STRATEGIC OPPORTUNITY-RISK, CAPABILITIES AND CATALYTIC ACTIONS MUST CONTINUOUSLY ALIGN WITH AND WITHIN CONDITIONS.

This is SiA. This is our algorithm. When you practice it as often as we do, it becomes second nature. It works as quickly as it needs to—which is to say, it works at the speed of disruption. Thinking SiA means thinking fast.

That's something that traditional planning processes don't allow for.

PLANNING IN SLOW MOTION

We make no bones about the fact that SiA is appreciably different from the traditional strategic planning process we've all grown to know and (frequently) loathe. SiA is specially designed for planning in an age of disruption, when connectivity, complexity, and chaos run at hyper-speeds on accelerating change cycles driven by new technology. Our experience is that traditional approaches to strategy just can't keep up. At best, they get us talking about where we'd like to go, but all too often, they result in irrelevant strategies that lack sufficient power and agility to inspire, align, and mobilize teams. Allow us to explain.

> **" TRADITION BECOMES OUR SECURITY, AND WHEN THE MIND IS SECURE IT IS IN DECAY."**
> *Jiddu Krishnamurti*

Traditional strategic plans run on five to ten year cycles. Like the Titanic, they are imposing, they eat up a lot of resources, and they're difficult to turn around once they get going. Generally, they revolve around three questions:

> *Where do we want to go?*
> *Where are we now?*
> *How do we close the gap from here to there?*

These questions are reasonable. They do a fairly good job of laying out the purpose of strategic planning. We all want particular outcomes and we need to contend with our present situation in order to get to where we want to go. The problem with the traditional strategic planning process is that it has taught us to treat these questions like disconnected pit stops on a racecourse to our desired outcomes.

Past, present, future: all neatly divided into their respective folders. If only it were so simple.

By now, it should be abundantly clear that this linear, plodding approach to planning reflects a bygone era. We are *not* living in the same world that gave rise to the stodgy strategic planning process we know and grudgingly put up with.

The modern strategic planning process entered business culture following World War II, when military leaders took tactical brainstorming to new heights. In the military, strategic planning was a process of determining desired outcomes, gathering intelligence, and planning (and trying to control) specific tactical maneuvers. Generals were thoroughly schooled in military history so that they could craft effective plans that were informed by precedent. What worked in the past was understood to be the most valid predictor of what would work in the present and future. After all, in the 1940s, the battleground of the past was not so very different from the battleground of the then-present or near future.

The business strategy culture that evolved from World War II to the 1980s reflects this attitude of sober deference to the past. The typical strategic planning process follows a careful series of steps so steeped in hoary tradition that the entire experience has taken on the character of a religious ritual. Define the vision, scan the environment, analyze the gaps, set goals, review progress, and repeat.

In this process, the "vision" is often based on a vanilla wish list that sounds exactly the same from organization to organization. The "plan" is contrived through an annual local environmental scan that is devoid of a timely, robust, and realistic understanding of the conditions facing the organization. And the resulting "projects" are lost in the mix as the day to day of real world conditions preoccupies the people meant to execute them.

PAUSE AND CONSIDER: *Think about your organization's "vision statement". Will it actually stand the true test of time?*

Moreover, this process tends to reinforce hierarchical business cultures that are also the legacy of militaristic history. Cumbersome five-year planning processes recruit select executives who are then charged with crafting a strategic vision in relative isolation. These executives run through their elaborate dance steps over tediously long periods of time, and by the time they take the stage, their performance may be totally out of synch with the reality that awaits them in the auditorium. Their team members watch disconnectedly, shrug, and then get back to it. They have work to do.

There is a reason why the very term "strategic planning" often evokes images of large binders gathering dust on shelves in executive offices. It is very difficult to create a traditional strategic plan that is relevant by the time it's ready to be executed. Relevant strategies are the product of teams who can think SiA in real-time, not executives who labor alone in hermetically sealed offices.

The thing is, even the military is beginning to agree with us. The best minds of the battlefield realize that 20th century methods of preparing, organizing, and executing strategy are outdated. When four-star general Stanley McChrystal, took over command of coalition forces in Afghanistan in 2004, it was plain to him that conventional military strategy was failing his forces.

To defeat Al Qaeda, he and his troops needed to adopt an operational style that matched the enemy's speed and flexibility. McChrystal divided his forces into a network of units with capabilities spread out globally. Each unit was empowered to act based on the conditions, opportunities, and risks that they perceived. They were, in McChrystal's words, a "team of teams". And in this flatter, faster, and more flexible formation, they were able to beat the enemy back.

LIZARD-BRAINS AND EMPTY SHELLS

If you want to better understand how SiA might diverge from the strategic planning processes of the past, why not consider the reptile?

> **❝ I WAS TAUGHT THAT THE HUMAN BRAIN WAS THE CROWNING GLORY OF EVOLUTION SO FAR, BUT I THINK IT'S A VERY POOR SCHEME FOR SURVIVAL.❞**
>
> *Kurt Vonnegut*

Reptiles emerge from their nativity baby-sized but essentially fully formed. They crack through the eggs in which they were gestated, leaving only empty shells behind, and quickly get on with the business of being reptiles. Their brains, devoid of limbic systems or executive functions, contain every instinct needed for governing a relatively simple set of behaviours. Eat, fight, flight, breed, and repeat. Learning really isn't part of the equation. Neither is creating new technology.

Mammals do it differently. When a mammal is born, it remains connected to and dependent upon its mother. The mother accompanies her infant, developing its complex mammalian brain long after birth. The quality of care a mammal receives—that is, how closely its mother delivers the feedback that stimulates learning—directly determines the success of that mammal's development. A good mother helps her baby to learn the behaviours that will help it to thrive in a milieu infinitely more complicated and nuanced than the "eat, fight, flight, breed, and repeat" world of the lizard.

Traditional strategic plans too often fall into a reptilian rut. When planners treat their newly born strategies like fully formed entities that are fit for any conditions, they are choosing to create dinosaurs.

On the other hand, strategies from a more advanced stage of evolution need their "mothers" to stay close. That is, the conditions that gave birth to the planning process (the first stage in SiA) remain a vital part of the ongoing development of the strategy in action. Conditions are seen as a living companion to SiA, a source of continual feedback, instruction, trim-tab, and change—strategy, *in action*.

Strategy for disruption is a cyclical process, running on real-time feedback. In SiA, the conditions that gave birth to the process keep informing a strategy that is elastic and responsive by nature.

Traditionalists like the old Kodak brass may say, "Our Komodo dragon is great, isn't it? It's big, tough, and eats everything in sight. It's the lord of this island! And all we had to do was hatch it and let it go."

Agile strategists say, "The environment is changing. This island is becoming inhospitable. We need to move. Good thing we have the advanced social organization skills to cross a land bridge into an entirely different continent. Thank god we are always evolving. Long live the Monkey Brain!"

Remember the First Principle. The steps of the SiA algorithm are bounded together in a cycle. We are not in the business of producing reptilian strategies that go forth to feed, kill, breed, flee, and repeat. We produce mammalian, evolved strategies that continuously receive feedback so that they can live and thrive in a more complex, globally connected, and chaotic environment where disruption is the rule, not the exception.

We do this because life is now moving much more quickly than a five-to-ten-year cycle can meaningfully account for. We do this because, like those football players, we realize we are players on a field of complex and rapid change, where skills—like strategies—cannot be robotically or ritualistically deployed. We are operating in a context of high impact, rapid-fire, and disruptive change, and we choose to be receptive to the feedback that allows for real-time adaptations. Once these components become misaligned—when, for example, the task of reading conditions is shucked off like so much Komodo dragon shell, or treated like the pit stop you passed ages ago—disaster is just around the corner. But if you learn to continually "check state", ensuring that your SiA is in alignment and oriented to the First Principle, you can make the real-time adaptations necessary for success.

What stage of evolution is your strategy at?

TRADE-IN THE TITANIC

For the past few centuries, organizations, businesses, networks, and communities of every description have been like vessels on a relatively calm, open sea. At one time, good seamanship meant maintaining the vessel: trimming sails, repairing the hull, swabbing the decks. The horizon rolled out in a predictable tableau, the maps were safely stowed below deck, and the ship's course had been plotted out long ago, probably on dry land. Of course these vessels had to weather squalls from time to time. But bad weather was the exception, not the rule.

We are now in an era when very little can be taken for granted. The weather has changed—permanently. Calm and predictable waters have given way to a battery of waves that continually grow in height and force. In this environment, maintaining the ship that crew and captain have grown to love and trust is no longer the end-goal. Sometimes, these seamen will have to use the materials of their ship to construct new vessels that can better navigate these waters. They will need agile and responsive capabilities that can leverage the power of the churning water, rather than fall prey to it. Seamen might even become surfers. To paraphrase Thomas Aquinas, if these captains decide, as Kodak's executives did, that their highest aim is to preserve their ships, they would be better off keeping them in port forever.

We know that it's possible to be at sea without being fatally pounded by the surf and overpowered by the weather. It's even possible to enjoy the ride if you have a vessel that allows you to continually course correct because you can really feel the dynamics of the water in your body at all times.

Reaping the rewards and managing the risks of disruptive change necessitates a framework for strategy that is more agile and responsive than the models of yesteryear. Thankfully, agility walks hand in hand with simplicity.

Meaning this need not be as difficult as it might sound.

Picture the Titantic. Now picture a surfboard. You are trading-in a monolith of the sea for a clean, lean, whittled-down instrument of travel.

What distinguishes SiA from the planning frameworks of the past is its emphasis on *changing ahead of change* and adapting in real-time. Basically, it entails keeping a few important habits in alignment. It's about balancing on a stack of ideas and practices that shape up as elegantly as a longboard cutting into a wall of surf.

DISRUPTION IS HERE. WHY NOT ENJOY THE RIDE?

CHAPTER 3

What Condition are my Conditions In?

LEARNING TO TAKE THE TEMPERATURE OF A FAST CHANGING WORLD

WHAT IT MEANS TO LAUNCH THE SIA ALGORITHM BY ASSESSING CONDITIONS, HOW TO BETTER UNDERSTAND THE GAPS IN YOUR KNOWLEDGE AND HOW FILLING THOSE GAPS CAN SAVE YOU FROM FALLING AFOUL OF DISRUPTION.

" FOR ME, GEOPOLITICAL ISSUES ARE BECOMING MORE IMPORTANT, BECAUSE HOW CAN YOU UNDERSTAND ECONOMY IF YOU DON'T UNDERSTAND GEOPOLITICS? PEOPLE THINK ECONOMISTS JUST DEAL WITH SPREADSHEETS AND CHARTS. THAT'S A NARROW-MINDED CARICATURE."

Nouriel Roubini

VOICES IN THE WILDERNESS

I n 2006, the economist Nouriel Roubini earned a nickname that never really sat right with him. On September 7th of that year, "Dr. Doom" took the stage at New York University to tell the economists of the International Monetary Fund that the American economy was in trouble. As he saw it, the housing market was teetering on the brink of oblivion, an oil shock was imminent, and consumer confidence would soon topple. He believed recession was coming and that it wasn't going to be the benign hiccup he knew most of his colleagues anticipated. Instead, he assured them it would be a "hard landing."

When he stepped down, there were sideways glances and muted titters. The consensus: Roubini was just being Roubini. A pathological pessimist. A man who lived to talk about worst-case scenarios. Besides, he was known to take an unconventional approach to analysis, relying less on mathematical models and more on a sweeping sense of historical precedent and global dynamics. His tack was all big-picture leaps and leftfield connections. He wasn't sufficiently grounded or data-driven.

A "hard landing"? Nobody bought it.

The same year Nouriel gave his doomsday address to the IMF, I (Larry) was living and working in a city on the American east coast. I had been teaching SiA principles to different groups in the city devoted to community and economic development. The need there was great. These were largely disenfranchised communities with high unemployment and low incomes. But there was a will to improve their and their family's futures. Many community members had migrated from poor countries and were living in the U.S. illegally. They usually held down two to three cash jobs just to make ends meet.

One day, I was leading one of these groups through the first step of the SiA algorithm: assessing conditions. The group talked about a range of forces affecting the quality of life and work in their community.

One participant spoke up: "You know, a lot of people here are being loaned money to buy homes they're not going to be able to afford in the long run." I questioned further and the phrase "predatory lending" emerged. Several others added their concerns about the practice.

Over the past 20 years I have personally completed close to a thousand conditions analyses. Often one condition sticks out from the rest. There are conditions that you can relate to all organizations, groups, or communities, and then there are the ones that deviate from the pattern, sometimes slightly and sometimes dramatically. *Wildcards.* This "predatory lending" wildcard was definitely an attention-grabber, so I decided to investigate further.

I discovered that the practice of sub-prime lenders pushing "no and low documentation" loans onto low socio-economic borrowers with little to no experience in taking on mortgages was rife in several of the communities and states I was working in. Basically borrowers were being either duped or "sold" into signing up for mortgages with dubious credit information. Worse, the mortgages had deferred interest payments that lulled the borrowers into a false sense of ownership and security. It was clear that they didn't have the means to buy a house and that when the actual interest rate kicked in and they were expected to pay, they would have little option but to default.

I also found out that this wasn't happening to the same extent in most other states, and relative to the total of these so-called "liar loans", the impact would register mostly at a local level. This would mean local pain as people were forced out of their new homes and onto the street. That was bad enough as it was, but as we now know, it was only the start of a truly massive disruption.

Over the next few months, I read articles in the *New York Times* that clearly illustrated something was up – and that the subprime fiasco was on its way from being a localized hardship to becoming a global disaster.

One article clearly laid out the coming crisis in plain language. Sub-prime loans had been bundled up with good loans into Collateralised Debt Obligations, which were then sold to global investors, and no one could really tell the good from the bad. The CDO market was going to hell in a hand basket. The final *New York Times* alert that got me was in the August 19, 2007 edition. In it, an infographic laid everything out, plain and simple. A global crisis was heading our way.

I approached banks, government authorities, and other stakeholders in the community with these concerns. I asked them, "How can we be resilient in the face of a collapse of the CDO market linked to sub-prime mortgages?"

I always got the same answer: "Why worry about *that*? It'll never happen."

One year later, almost to the day, the global financial crisis was upon us. By this time I was back in Australia. I remember watching a television program in September 2008 when the bubble burst and all hell broke loose. The CEO of a major Australian bank defended the loss of $2 billion of shareholder funds with that clarion call of M.A.D.: "No one could have reasonably foreseen these circumstances."

If I had a brick on hand, I would have thrown it at the television.

THE THREAT OF DISCONTINUITY

We've discussed exponential change. We've pictured the world as a highly connected, complex and chaotic network experiencing accelerating change cycles. And even though we're incapable of truly plumbing the depths of this era of disruptive change in a book of this length, we chose to dip our toes in, to see if the water is inviting or not at this stage. From Wilson's 3-D printed Liberator, to globalization's proactive 13%, we've skimmed through some of the broader trends that should drive the reality of this exponentially disruptive era home to you.

If continuity is our desired state—continually generating value, growing the bottom line, living long and prospering—then discontinuity—running off the tracks, defaulting or bankrupting, melting down or giving up—is our worst-case scenario. Could there be a more definitive example of discontinuity rearing its ugly head than the sub-prime crisis and what followed: the global economy running off the rails, strewing passengers and cargo as far as the eye could see?

The story of the sub-prime crisis's lonely voices in the wilderness drives another point home: if we truly desire continuity we had better listen up and watch out. No matter how choppy the waters get, we believe in our capacity to prepare. There is simply no need to lose big and then resort to saying, "Nobody could have seen it coming."

" THIS MANDATE THAT I SEEK IS ABOUT CONTINUITY AND SUSTAINABILITY AGAINST DISRUPTION AND STAGNATION, ABOUT MOVING FORWARD VERSUS REGRESSING. WE HAVE TO SAFEGUARD WHAT WE HAVE ALREADY ACHIEVED. WE CANNOT PUT AT RISK WHAT WE HAVE; WE CANNOT GAMBLE AWAY OUR FUTURE."

Najib Razak

Continuity begins with reading the signs and receiving the signals—and more signs and signals than you might be in the habit of taking in. It certainly means paying closer attention to those voices in the wilderness, even when their outlook seems offensively bearish, or informed by sources that strike you as out-there, abstract, or counter-intuitive. Sometimes, these are the only perspectives that are big-picture enough to catch what nobody else does.

PAUSE AND CONSIDER: *When was the last time you heard an out-there prediction that came true? At the time when you first learned about it, did you ignore it or take it seriously? Why or why not?*

In the last chapter, we introduced the simple algorithm that is SiA, that step-by-step mental maneuver that, with practice, becomes an athletic state of mind. Now, we are ready to discuss the first stage of SiA in more detail. We are ready to discuss conditions, that all-important mammalian mother of agile strategies-in-action, that dimension of the strategy process that makes everything else *make sense*. We are ready to discuss reading the signs and receiving the signals as our first step to planning for brilliant continuity.

THE ACTOR DISGUISED AS A BACKDROP

First of all, what do we mean by "conditions"? The Oxford Dictionary explains that *conditions* are the "state of something, especially with regard to its appearance or working order", or to a "set of circumstances" that determines the way people live or work. But then again, adds Dictionary, we could always be using it as a verb, in which case we might be talking about

" *MY FOREGROUNDS ARE IMAGINARY, MY BACKGROUNDS REAL.* "

Gustave Flaubert

"exercising a significant influence on outcomes". A dog's *condition* might be poor, sick, and old after years of digging in the dirt, sleeping outside, and chasing small animals in all sorts of *conditions*. Or it might be *conditioned* to sit when it is given a treat.

PAUSE AND CONSIDER: *Think fast... how would you answer a five-year-old child who walked up to you and asked, "What does 'conditions' mean?"*

We appreciate the fact that the word "condition" is a noun as well as a verb, because it underscores something important about the concept. That is, a condition could be a state of affairs that merely provides context, a backdrop against which various performances play out. But then, all of a sudden, that backdrop in our theatrical production might grow arms and limbs, and clamber forward onto the stage, demanding to play a role. "Conditions" might appear to be static. In reality they are dynamic players. They are both noun and verb.

Conditions, like the weather, can be ignored or taken for granted before suddenly manifesting as forces to be reckoned with. They are both the sunny days that call people out of their office buildings and apartments, and the sudden downpours that ruin the picnics. As Negroponte explains: they are a " trickle that becomes a downpour". When you start wrapping your mind around conditions, it's very important to remember this duality. Remember the noun-and-verb-ness of conditions.

CLASSIFYING CONDITIONS

Obviously, we (and our trusty dictionary) cut a very wide swathe with our use of the term "conditions". We know that makes the concept seem a little overwhelming. Is there any limit to the number of factors that impact your organization or define its state of being? How do we begin to think meaningfully about a concept so potentially gargantuan?

IN SIA, WE BREAK IT DOWN LIKE THIS:

Immediate and Emergent

Start by thinking of conditions as both immediate (an actor strolling around stage, influencing the current storyline) and emergent (scenery hanging out at the back of a very large stage, so far away that it might be a bit difficult to make out). The immediate is happening now, and the emergent may or will occur in the future. Consider the weather. We have the weather right now—sunny skies, warm temperature, a perfect picnic setting—and we have the weather that's rolling in over the horizon—for example, dark clouds bearing picnic-disrupting precipitation.

Micro, Macro and Mega

Next, realize that conditions are best thought about as occurring at different scales. To make the task of parsing out different kinds of conditions a little easier, and to get us thinking about conditions that aren't immediately impacting us or defining our state of affairs, we think about the micro, macro, and mega levels where conditions reside.

The Micro level is the space you and your organization occupy. Your micro may resemble the micros of others in particular ways, but it's essentially a unique space. You and the people around you are in your own cluster of conditions and change cycles that hook into the broader network in idiosyncratic ways, at your own particular pace. The conditions you experience—for example, low staff turnover, a high concentration of information technology savvy people, a languishing sales force, an imminently retiring CEO—define a micro unlike any other. In this micro-space, you are most sensitive to and aware of conditions.

IMMEDIATE   EMERGENT

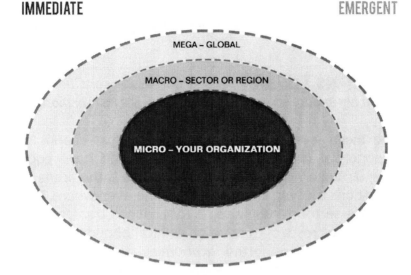

Diagram 3.1 | **THE MICRO, MACRO AND MEGA OF CONDITIONS**

The immediate and emergent conditions impacting an organization are best thought about as occurring at different scales.

Here, you are most likely to perceive conditions and call them by their names.

PAUSE AND CONSIDER: *Name one micro-condition that is having a big impact on you today.*

The Macro level is where your conditions are similar to those of a broader and deeper set. Macro is where sector, regional and national forces play out. An election that transforms the composition of government, a new law impacting how you and your sector do business, a new competitor, a protest movement that starts influencing key decision-makers in various regions—these conditions define your macro level experience. You read about these developments in the paper and discuss them at dinner parties. You are still likely to be aware of conditions at the macro level, but less acutely than you are of micro-conditions.

PAUSE AND CONSIDER: *Name one macro-condition that had a big impact on your organization in the last six months.*

The Mega level is where you can spy that chariot of exponential change rumbling along if you have good long distance vision. Mega is Global. This is the arena of conditions that you share with everyone, everywhere. This is where sector trends sweep across nations, transforming life without respect to state or political boundaries. This is where interconnected economies and information systems define generational trends. This is where a single technological breakthrough can produce a multitude of spin-off effects, ushering us into a radically new era. Obviously, in this rarefied mega-space, it becomes increasingly more challenging to practice awareness of conditions. As the levels of conditions radiate outward, becoming larger and more abstract, your eyesight strains, your comprehension wanes. In the Mega, an appetite for a broad view outside of your comfort zone is a must if you want to keep abreast of conditions. This is where you need plenty of intentional practice and eyes other than your own to be on the lookout for the game-changers and wildcards.

Remember that the global financial crisis started at a local level, went national, and then global before you or your organization felt its local effects. And failure to actively monitor the mega conditions of this globalized, digitally connected, and transacted world will only have greater consequences in the years ahead.

PAUSE AND CONSIDER: *Name one emergent mega-condition that could have a big impact on your organization in the next few years.*

Value Neutral

Finally—and this is crucial—throw out any system you may already have for classifying conditions. Most people seem accustomed to slotting conditions into two categories: "Good" or "Bad."

That is an unhelpful way to view conditions. It just gets in the way of sound decision-making.

We've learned to treat conditions without judgment. They are the "what is". Remember when we spoke about chaos and suggested that one person's discontinuity is another person's continuity? Or, that a negative experience of discontinuity could just as easily be positive? As with the forest fire from Chapter 2, you could choose to perceive any given condition as either a force of environmental destruction or renewal. Both could be true. You could make a good argument either way. Yet, fundamentally, the fire just is. It's worth getting out of the habit of labeling conditions with the broad strokes of "good" or "bad", because doing so will cloud your thinking. It will either lull you into a false sense of imminent, can't-go-wrong opportunity or activate a debilitating anxiety that causes you to fixate on risks, or worse—lay down and accept your fate long before it's been sealed.

The message here is: understand the conditions and don't create self-fulfilling prophecies.

PAUSE AND CONSIDER: *Name one condition you have the habit of labeling as "bad" that could actually be a positive opportunity, or a disruption you could leverage.*

Does breaking the habit of labeling conditions strike you as a tall order? What can we say? Evolution isn't easy. The goods news is that SiA can make that evolution easier. Which leads us to *Thinking Conditions*.

THINKING CONDITIONS

In 2002, when Donald Rumsfeld was quizzed by reporters about the apparent lack of evidence linking the Iraqi government to terrorist groups, he famously responded with a koan so torturous, he was given the "Foot in Mouth" award from the Plain Language Campaign. Against a backdrop of fear and loathing in the build up to the Iraqi War, he mused about the possibility of a sworn enemy of the American people harboring weapons of mass destruction, saying:

> *" THERE IS NO LOGICAL WAY TO THE DISCOVERY OF THESE ELEMENTAL LAWS. THERE IS ONLY THE WAY OF INTUITION, WHICH IS HELPED BY A FEELING FOR THE ORDER LYING BEHIND THE APPEARANCE."*
>
> Albert Einstein

Reports that say that something hasn't happened are always interesting to me, because as we know, there are known knowns; there are things we know we know. We also know there are known unknowns; that is to say we know there are some things we do not know. But there are also unknown unknowns—the ones we don't know we don't know. And if one looks throughout the history of our country and other free countries, it is the latter category that tends to be the difficult ones.

Geopolitical subterfuge aside, we can't help but doff our caps to Rumsfeld over this distillation of a terrifically subtle concept sometimes referred to as "the field of all knowledge". Although we can appreciate the concerns of the Plain Language warriors, the fact is that Rumsfeld was right. Not about the weapons of mass destruction, of course. (About the weapons: dead wrong.) But his taxonomy of knowledge types, on the other hand, is pretty astute. Perhaps philosophy just doesn't go over so well in a heated Department of Defense briefing.

Think about it this way: if you could do as Rumsfeld did and represent all that you know and do not know as a pie chart carved into different sections, how would you label the pieces, and how large would each one be? We think it might look something like this:

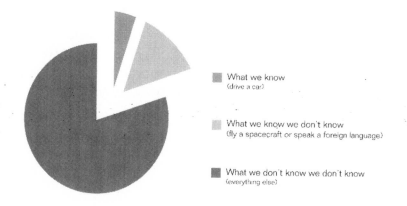

What we know
(drive a car)

What we know we don't know
(fly a spacecraft or speak a foreign language)

What we don't know we don't know
(everything else)

Diagram 3.2 | **THE FIELD OF ALL KNOWLEDGE**

The Field of All Knowledge is a concept designed to illustrate all of the knowledge available to us, in a simple diagram.

Each mind carries around a storehouse with different compartments. There's what you know, what you think you know, what you know you don't know, and what you don't know you don't know. And Rumsfeld is entirely right when he says (admittedly a bit cryptically) that the last compartment tends to contain the "difficult ones", the pieces of information that sweep out of left-field, catching us unawares and unprepared. Bombs from Baghdad. Yes, these "unknown unknowns" are indeed interesting.

So what's the point of trying to take this birds-eye view of your own mind? Aren't these concepts a little on the abstract side? Are you reacting with a certain amount of impatience, like those nonplussed reporters at the Department of Defense briefing?

Well, as we've stressed a few times already, SiA is about rethinking your approach to strategy so that it is more agile and responsive in the disruptive age. And this boils down to upgrading the way you *think*. Remember that this is about muscle memory on a dynamic field of play, not elaborate rituals in a hermetically sealed executive office. So while "thinking about thinking" can get us into some airy philosophical territory, it's a very important step to take if you want to start *thinking* SiA, which is to say, strategizing at the speed of disruption.

What we're asking you to do is take a minute to acknowledge how much you *don't know*. The first step to recovery is admitting you have a problem.

Next, acknowledge that what you *think* you know can also be a problem. Like those IMF economists using mathematical models to justify their expectation of a "soft landing", sometimes you have no idea how difficult it is for you to actually grasp the reality of your situation. You can hardly help it—you're rigged that way.

The cognitive scientist Andrew Shtulman recently showed that even an advanced scientific education never completely eliminates our attachment to false beliefs that *feel* true. He conducted a study in which he asked university-level science students whether the Earth travels around the sun. They were also asked whether the moon travels around the Earth. The students tended to answer both questions correctly but they paused when answering questions that challenged their sense of intuition, or "naïve beliefs." After all, it *looks* like both the sun and moon travel around the Earth.

In the case of the sun, we are asked to believe something that is not self-evident, because science has confirmed that, in this case, our eyes deceive us. Shtulman's research suggests that even when we are armed with scientifically verified facts, if they are not intuitive—if our senses and felt experience don't confirm them—we will always subconsciously struggle just a little bit to believe these facts.

Remember the cognitive biases we described in Chapter 1? What about our tendency to revert to Fixed Action Patterns? Or our predisposition to ignore the exponential because we expect a stimulus to deliver an immediate effect? There are so many reasons why we struggle to come to grips with evidence that flies in the face of what we think we already know.

When Dr. Doom rolled out his stormy vision of the near future, the American economy was still in growth mode. Unemployment and inflation were low. Now, oil prices *were* up and the housing market *had* started to decline moderately, but these developments hardly seemed like harbingers of an economic meltdown. For the majority of economists in Roubini's audience, all signs pointed towards mild recession, a slight dip in an overarching pattern of robust growth. What Roubini was asking them to believe was utterly counter-intuitive. It strained all credulity.

M.A.D. flourishes in organizational cultures that fail to acknowledge and understand counter-intuitive insights that strain all credulity but happen to be *true*. Organizations that point myopically to short-term growth patterns and ignore the squalls over the horizon are squarely in the zone of M.A.D. Like those Collateralized Debt Obligations, these organizations look good, but they're very likely rotten to the core. Without a perspective that is plugged into emergent conditions—that rarefied abstract space Roubini was known to travel—it's all too easy to justify complacency by pointing to the favorable present. Although your organization needs to be grounded in "the facts" of the present moment, it also needs to create a safe place for intuition, for the type of thinking that makes inspired connections between disparate elements.

You and your team need to be on the active lookout for "wild cards" at all scales. Scan the horizon for those conditions that swoop in from leftfield, radiating into your micro from the mega level, or vice versa. These conditions originate as weak signals from the realm of the "unknown unknowns" and they matter more than you might think.

PAUSE AND CONSIDER: *Where can you see Managed Adaptive Decline creeping into your organization in the form of denial of emergent conditions? Which out-there intuitions and connections represent "wild cards" that might matter more than you want to consider?*

Recognize that we are all operating with an information deficit of some type. Even what you *think* you know might be flawed in some fatal way. The fact is that the "unknown unknowns" are impacting your experience and that of your organization without even making an impression on your conscious mind. From time to time, your senses will deceive you into a false sense of security that could breed M.A.D. if you aren't careful.

You will occasionally find the truth to be elusive, counter-intuitive, or too "out there" to easily assimilate. You may also identify another type of file in your "unknown unknowns" folder, the "I technically know it but I don't want to know it." That's ok. Once again, admitting there is a problem is the first step to getting help. And where does this help come from?

IT'S ALL AROUND YOU.

CREATING A CULTURE OF THINKING CONDITIONS

When Abby Harris[1] first started as the CEO of an alternative fuel industry association, she gave them six months. If they couldn't create a reasonable strategic plan together in that timeframe, she'd be on her way. The association had not had a CEO in place for half a year. Their board and leadership were at frequent odds over strategic direction. They didn't seem to have a relevant or clear value proposition. As Harris puts it, "They just weren't having a sophisticated conversation about strategy."

Harris was introduced to Resilient Futures some years earlier, and what she'd learned about SiA stuck with her. So when she began the tough work of pushing her association out of its malaise, she called. Five months of stakeholder interviews and information-gathering later, we sat down with the Board. Based on the rich overview the Conditions Analysis provided, the true value proposition of the association suddenly seemed starkly self-evident—and it was very different from the one everyone had been talking about.

What this team realized was that they had been neglecting to take the pulse of macro conditions, which happened to be exerting a considerable influence on their state of affairs. Political shifts and policy developments on the horizon were crying out for their attention. They had been arguing about their association when they needed to have a conversation about their industry. As a result of their newfound clarity, they swiftly identified key projects for the coming year. Even though these projects required additional funding, they easily secured the money from their funders because they were able to demonstrate credible evidence supporting the value they realized they could generate for stakeholders.

---

1   This name has been changed to protect privacy.

"Thinking Conditions" gave the association new momentum and allowed them to create a new culture. When policy changes came down the pipeline they met them with a purposeful and prepared attitude. As Harris puts it, "Suddenly, they had a reason *why*."

If there is much that you don't know, don't see, and don't understand, you run a high risk of running off-course and inflicting grievous discontinuity on yourself. What are you supposed to do about that exposure? How can you safeguard yourself against self-imposed ignorance and shortsightedness? Even if you learn to pay better attention to immediate and emergent conditions, how can you possibly stay on top of all there is to know in this disruptive age of complex and exponentially accelerating changes?

The first thing you need to know is that you can't go it alone. A conventional environmental scan relegated to the executive office won't cut muster. You need a team—as big and diverse a team as you can harness, both within and extending outside of your organization. A team of listeners, watchers, and thinkers. Many minds make light work. In organizations that practice SiA, there is a culture of "thinking conditions." These teams are accustomed to monitoring immediate and emergent conditions at scale and sharing what they know so that they can collectively reduce their "unknown unknowns".

PAUSE AND CONSIDER: *How many people from diverse backgrounds are involved with discussions about conditions or strategy in your organization?*

In Resilient Futures we have a saying that reinforces the power of an array of listening posts feeding back information: "The network always knows. If it doesn't, then there's something wrong with the network." In today's informed and connected world, there is someone, somewhere, who knows what you need to know. And given our reality of "three degrees of separation", they aren't hard to find.

Beyond seeing further and learning more, teams who map conditions together also develop a shared context for decision-making. A group of people who have "seen the light" together are much more likely to achieve consensus, design strategies, and execute initiatives that inspire all team members equally. This team argues less but communicates more. Groupthink gives way to dialogue.

We see evidence that an organization has developed a culture of conditions and a shared context for decision-making when we start to observe team members asking each other questions like: "Do we have anybody in our network who could help us to make a better decision?" Or: "Are there any emergent conditions that could impact the action we're thinking about taking?"

IT IS A POWERFUL THING TO BEHOLD.

MAPPING & MONITORING CONDITIONS

When we teach the first stage of the SiA algorithm, helping an organization to create a culture of conditions, we talk about mapping and monitoring. The focus is on aligning around a shared understanding of conditions—and then continually refreshing that view so that it always reflects real-time conditions.

This starts with the creation of a Conditions Map. This Map is a visual and verbal representation of the various conditions that are defining the organization's current and emergent state of affairs. It identifies the primary conditions existing at the micro, macro, or mega scale.

When the Map is completed, it looks something like this:

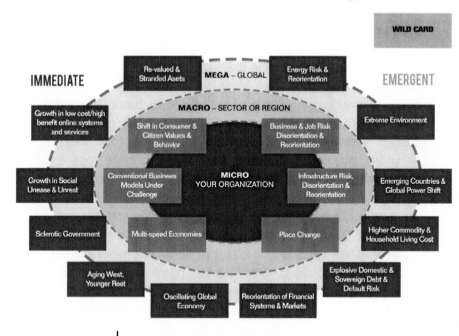

Diagram 3.3 | **A CONDITIONS MAP**

A Conditions Map is a visual and verbal representation of the various conditions that are defining an organization's immediate and emergent state of affairs. It identifies the primary conditions existing at the micro, macro, or mega scale. This example identified by Resilient Futures is a map of key global conditions, occurring at the macro and mega scales.

This Map is the product of a diverse team working together to collect and pool knowledge. This team taps into a diverse network of listening posts—contacts, stakeholders, media sources, specialists, thought leaders, wild cards and voices in the wilderness—to build a rich overview of their organization's situation in the world. We call this a 360-degree perspective, and it's different from what you gain from a mere environmental scan or SWOT analysis. It is more nuanced, more complete. It reaches further to discover conditions that are not judged as either "good" or "bad".

PAUSE AND CONSIDER: *Name one person you never considered consulting on a regular basis in order to get a fuller sense of your organization's immediate and emergent conditions. How do they connect with what you do? How could you take measures to stay in touch?*

Most importantly, the team that can create this kind of Map is the team that talks together about what matters. It's a team that comes to crucial consensus, just like Harris's association learned to do. Monitoring of conditions becomes an intrinsic part of their thinking and perspective. Their Map is a snapshot of the team's shared perspective and underpins every strategic decision they need to make. This empowers the team to move swiftly when the conditions emerge and the timing is right. No need for lengthy debate. They already possess a foundation for agile action.

Once a Map is in place, we must always remember the First Principle:

To generate sustainable value, strategic opportunity-risk, capabilities and catalytic actions must continuously align with and within conditions.

That is, our pursuit of opportunities, management of risk, assertion of value generation, and investment in capability doesn't matter or make sense unless all of it is in alignment with conditions. That means constantly hitting the "refresh button" on the dashboard displaying our view of shifting conditions. After all, what happens when we are out of alignment with conditions—that is to say, with reality? Discontinuity rears its ugly head. We go off track. We become disoriented, like Harris's team bickering about strategic "vision" under the auspices of an irrelevant value proposition. Our capacity to generate authentic and sustainable value is destroyed.

Hence, constant monitoring must follow mapping. We stay connected to our listening posts and build our culture of conditions in both informal and formal ways. Perhaps a dedicated Conditions Team meets regularly to hit that refresh button on the Conditions Map. Perhaps we make a habit of asking questions outside of our micro bubble, drawing upon the insights of our suppliers, customers, association members, or community members. This is a dynamic culture, not a work project, so we do not relegate our Map or our Conditions Analysis to a folder in an executive office, never to revisit it.

DOCTORS OF REALISM

In 2006, two years prior to the global financial crisis, when Dr. Doom was making his thunderous prognostications and I was asking my peculiar questions in a rather less public setting, there were most certainly other voices in the wilderness chiming in. Those who were naturally "thinking conditions" could see the threat of discontinuity on the horizon.

> **" TRUE REALISM CONSISTS IN REVEALING THE SURPRISING THINGS WHICH HABIT KEEPS COVERED AND PREVENTS US FROM SEEING."**
>
> Jean Cocteau

But there were far more people who preferred to play the ostrich, content to let mysterious forces play out in the realm of "unknown unknowns." The sunny present moment suited them just fine, and they spread their blankets out for a picnic.

Roubini is known to take issue with his cartoon-villain nickname, claiming that he's no pessimist by nature. He believes that his big picture perspective and sensitivity to risk makes him a realist. Nothing more, nothing less.

For my part, my investigations in that small American city were fueled by a habit of asking questions when I didn't have the answers. I recognized the limits of my knowledge, and filled in the gaps by connecting with my network. Nothing more, nothing less.

You need not be a genius with a cartoon villain name to "think conditions." You need not be omniscient or eerily intuitive to spy what might be rolling over the horizon. You just need to plug into the resources all around you. You need to recognize that you are not alone. Because of that, you have no excuse.

Disruption Readiness Checklist #1

A quick way to take your pulse on your readiness for disruption is to ask the following questions with respect to your organization. Remember that each chapter will add a few more questions to your checklist ensuring that you are fully disruption-ready by the end.

☐ We understand that conditions are both immediate and emergent but always value-neutral.

☐ We map out the immediate and emergent conditions impacting our organization today and tomorrow at the micro, macro, and mega scales.

☐ We continually monitor these conditions and "hit refresh" on our conditions map by staying connected to a network of listening posts.

☐ We include listening posts that give us "wild card" information, make intuitive connections between disparate information sources, and help us to reduce our "unknown unknowns".

CHAPTER 4 | Heads or Tails?

PURSUING STRATEGIC OPPORTUNITY-RISKS

DEFINING A STRATEGIC OPPORTUNITY-RISK, HOW IT FITS INTO THE SIA ALGORITHM, AND HOW STEVE JOBS AND HIS TEAM PERCEIVED AND PURSUED THE STRATEGIC OPPORTUNITY-RISKS THAT SAVED APPLE FROM BANKRUPTCY AND MADE IT A DEFINING PLAYER IN THIS ERA OF DISRUPTION.

" *LET THE FUTURE TELL THE TRUTH, AND EVALUATE EACH ONE ACCORDING TO HIS WORK AND ACCOMPLISHMENTS. THE PRESENT IS THEIRS; THE FUTURE, FOR WHICH I HAVE REALLY WORKED, IS MINE.*"

NIKOLA TESLA

THINK DIFFERENT

In Kodak's *annus horribilus* of 2012, when it was forced to declare Chapter 11 Bankruptcy, it held a fire sale. With the assistance of intellectual property aggregators RPX and Intellectual Ventures, it drummed up about $525 Million USD for approximately 1,100 digital imaging and processing patents.

The patents had been reportedly valued at $2.5 Billion, but Kodak wasn't in any position to bargain.

So who ponied up for Kodak's storehouse of great (if unexecuted) ideas? The consortium of buyers included this disruptive age's newly minted elite, tech titans like Google and Facebook. Most symbolic of all, Apple was among them, happy to collect Kodak's intellectual property at a discounted price, like a poker player who had placed all the right bets.

If Kodak sealed its fate by holding onto the past, Apple built its empire by predicting the future—and then creating it before anyone else could. This is why Apple's tagline "Think Different" now has the resonance of a quasi-religious mantra for many people living in an era of exponential change.

In 1997, the year Apple launched the "Think Different" campaign, the company was on the verge of bankruptcy.

Sales had fallen from $11 billion USD in 1995 to $7 billion USD that year. After an eight-year exile from the company he founded, Steve Jobs was back at the helm as CEO. At a Macworld Expo conference on August 6th, he spoke candidly about the situation Apple was in and what he intended to do about it:

> *I came today to give you a status report on what's going on and to try to fill you in on some of the steps we're taking to get Apple healthy again. Apple's not as relevant as it used to be everywhere, but in some incredibly important market segments it's extraordinarily relevant.*

> *Apple is executing wonderfully on many of the wrong things. The ability of the organization to execute is really high, though. I mean I've met some extraordinary people at Apple. There's a lot of great people at Apple. They're doing some of the wrong things because the plan has been wrong. What I found is rather than anarchy, I found people who can't wait to fall into line behind a good strategy. There just hasn't been one. [...]*

> *Apple needs to find where it is still incredibly relevant and focus on those areas. It needs to figure out what its core assets are and invest more in them. Apple has neglected its core assets for a while. It has to forge some meaningful partnerships, not just partnerships and press releases. And it needs to define some new product paradigms.*

Clearly, the "Think Different" campaign was a poetic volley launched by Job's hard-nosed assessment of Apple's situation in the mid-nineties. He seemed to understand where the hope lay. He believed he had the right people. Apple's issue wasn't operational. They didn't need to just dig in and work harder. Rather, they needed a "good strategy." For Jobs, that boiled down to two components:

defining "new product paradigms" and then building those products for the "incredibly important market segments" for which Apple was "extraordinarily relevant."

When Jobs unveiled "Think Different" to his staff at an internal meeting on September 23rd, 1997, he explained it like this: "What we're about isn't making boxes for people to get their jobs done. Although we do that well. We do that better than almost anybody in some cases. But Apple's about something more than that. Apple at the core...our core value is that we believe that people with passion can change the world for the better."

THE STRATEGY, THEN, WAS CLEAR. CHANGE THE WORLD.

FROM MAKING BOXES TO MAKING CULTURE

Few in 1997 could have foreseen how thoroughly Apple would make good on its promise to change the world. Indeed, in a few short years, Apple completely reinvented itself, and in doing so, reinvented the world, becoming a hugely significant driver in the network of accelerating change cycles we call the disruptive era. Their line of ingeniously user-friendly devices and associated platforms ushered our culture into a radically new arena of digital technology and smart device dominance. And it was an arena that Apple was able to rule from the outset because it was responsible for defining the new product paradigm that Jobs promised.

> **" EVERYONE HERE HAS THE SENSE THAT RIGHT NOW IS ONE OF THOSE MOMENTS WHEN WE ARE INFLUENCING THE FUTURE."**
>
> Steve Jobs

Jobs was right: ultimately, Apple was not about "making boxes." If Kodak was in the camera-and-film production business, Apple was up to something else entirely. But what exactly was that?

Now, we are a hero-worshipping culture, so we're predisposed to bestow Jobs with godlike capabilities. Just like with Dr. Doom, we have transformed Steve Jobs into a cartoonish hero who operated in a realm too rarefied for ordinary folk. Although in many ways it's natural, it's also a way of letting ourselves off of the hook. "Nobody could have seen things the way he saw them" is after all just a different way of expressing that mantra of M.A.D.: "Nobody could have seen it coming."

In the interest of curbing our own tendencies towards M.A.D. hero worship, why don't we just *try* seeing things the way Jobs and his team saw them in 1997. Whatever it was, it wasn't a vision of the future Jobs beheld in a crystal ball.

What Apple *did* see in the mid-nineties is something we call a Strategic Opportunity-Risk (SOR). It was opportunity arising out of real-world conditions. It embedded a certain level of risk but also a lot of potential for explosive growth. Finally, it was an opportunity that Jobs' people needed to strategically pursue in order to achieve. It was never going to fall into their laps, no matter how much of a genius their leader was.

But before we unpack Apple's specific SOR and how its pursuit led to the fulfillment of Jobs' most soaring rhetoric, let's unpack the term itself.

DEFINING STRATEGIC OPPORTUNITY-RISK

A Strategic Opportunity-Risk is a set of conditions providing for both progress *and* exposure to danger that will strategically position an organization to generate sustainable value. Let's break this down.

> " *ALL MEN CAN SEE THESE TACTICS WHEREBY I CONQUER, BUT WHAT NONE CAN SEE IS THE STRATEGY OUT OF WHICH VICTORY IS EVOLVED.*"
>
> Sun Tzu

Emerging from Conditions

We look to conditions to find SORs. The immediate and emergent factors playing out at the micro, macro, and mega levels provide the substance of SORs. SORs are like the constellations we can perceive in a sky full of stars. When you take the time to map out your conditions and contemplate how they might connect, these shapes can sometimes stand out very clearly and suddenly, the way they did for Abby Harris and her team in Chapter 3.

PAUSE AND CONSIDER: *Do your organization's strategic opportunities seem more obvious when you look into the micro, macro, or mega conditions? Does looking at these conditions together reveal clearer patterns of opportunity?*

Risk and Opportunity: Two Sides of a Single Coin

A SOR provides both the potential for progress and exposure to danger. Remember when we encouraged you to break the habit of judging conditions as good or bad? This is where non-judgment really comes into play. As much as we all might enjoy the idea of a cut-and-dried reality, a world of villains and heroes, if you persist in seeing conditions this way, you're choosing to cloud your strategic vision. Like Nouriel Roubini, you need to be a Dr. Reality. And the reality is this: any opportunity embeds a certain level of risk, and any risk embeds a certain level of opportunity. The two are inseparable, like the two sides of a single coin. One person's opportunity is always another person's risk. Even in a disruptive environment. If Kodak perceived digital imaging technology as a profound risk, Apple perceived it as a tremendous opportunity.

For this reason, we choose to combine "opportunity" and "risk" into a single term, "opportunity-risk". It helps us to remember we are always simultaneously leveraging a certain level of opportunity and managing or mitigating a certain level of risk when we pick a strategic target and begin moving towards it. This prevents us from being either too Pollyanna-ish or too fearful. Risk-fixation can turn you into a Kodak, but it's also entirely possible to be so convinced that an opportunity is a surefire winner that you fail to prepare yourself for the inevitable hazards you will encounter en route to collecting your winnings. When you keep opportunity and risk in focus, you give yourself the best chance of generating sustainable value inside of a particular set of conditions.

PAUSE AND CONSIDER: *Do the opportunities revealed through your view of your organization's conditions strike you as particularly risky? Name one risk that comes to mind.*

Active Pursuit of SORs Generates Sustainable Value

The point of all of this is to generate sustainable value. Note that we take pains to say "sustainable" value. In 1975, when Kodak's Steve Sasson invented the digital camera, Kodak was generating tremendous value. But much of this value was ultimately unsustainable, given emergent conditions. While other companies invested heavily into "filmless photography" that began as a Kodak innovation, Kodak was quite happy to continue gobbling up market share as a film-and-camera company. After all, there was plenty of market share to go around at that time. They looked at their digital innovation through black-and-white glasses and perceived only danger. They saw the coin of SOR spinning through the air and only noticed the risk side. They slotted digital into the "bad" file and set themselves firmly against it.

For a long time, their market dominance seemed to vindicate their approach. They were an American institution. They seemed "too big to fail." In fact in 1999, two years after Apple entreated us all to "Think Different", Kodak's stock prices were higher than they had ever been, with shares priced at nearly $80 USD. Kodak looked good but their value was rotting from the inside, as decayed as those Collateralized Debt Obligations were in the sub-prime heyday.

In other words, Kodak was the very picture of M.A.D. They lost the ability to generate sustainable value and eventually it showed.

PAUSE AND CONSIDER: *Is your organization generating sustainable value? Or is it running the risk of going M.A.D.?*

You Must Actively Pursue SORs

The failure to actively pursue the right SORs results in going slowly but surely M.A.D. When you try to shove an SOR into the closet, like Kodak did with Sasson's camera, it doesn't stay put. It reappears as an immense problem, a punch that knocks you sideways. You are not able to generate sustainable value as a static entity that invests only into its own maintenance. Like a surfer, you must constantly maneuver yourself into the right wave at the right moment. If you wait, drop your anchor, and try to "sit out" exponential change, you will experience the fully expressed destructive potential of its wave. What does it feel like to have the future hammering down on you from above?

Move forward. You don't have a choice.

Both continuity and discontinuity mean generating value despite—or because of—shifts in conditions. Your own experience of this depends on your ability to make out the shape of SORs in your immediate and emergent conditions and then orient yourself towards the right ones. After all, the state of generating sustainable value is the opposite of M.A.D.

In Terms of SiA

When you are first learning SiA, identifying SORs is the second step of the SiA algorithm. (After you've mastered the algorithm, identifying SORs is something you do continually as the wheel of SiA keeps turning.)

Since SORs are substantiated by conditions, we begin to understand what they are once we've mapped our immediate and emergent conditions at scale. A SOR can be based on a single condition or seen as a cluster of conditions that appear like a footprint in the micro, macro, and mega conditions of your organization. It's like a beam from a flashlight that shows you where you might go and what you might do in order to generate value. In terms of the football player analogy, "identifying a SOR" is the moment you perceive an undefended space in front of the goal. You realize you could capitalize on it if you only took a few steps to the right and kicked hard with the inside of your right boot.

As always, remember the First Principle of SiA: *to generate sustainable value, opportunity-risk, capabilities and actions must continuously align with and within conditions.* The SOR is only valid—that is, it will only generate sustainable value—when it is aligned with conditions. If another player suddenly blocks that space, your conditions have changed, and you need to re-think your SOR and adjust your catalytic actions (run, kick, pass, pivot) accordingly.

When your SiA is disoriented from the First Principle then discontinuity and value destruction will follow. This is tantamount to a player kicking the ball straight to the opponent who has just crossed his path, rather than into the goal as he intended. It's a goal lost and a player that's been properly disrupted.

PAUSE AND CONSIDER: *Can you think of another analogy for how SORs fit into the SiA algorithm?*

Apple's Strategic Opportunity-Risk

Now that we've properly defined a SOR, we can return to the work of removing the superhero's cape from the great Mr. Jobs, and trying to see what he and his team saw in 1997. What was the SOR that Apple's understanding of conditions revealed at that pivotal moment in the history of their organization?

Jobs' August 6th Macworld Expo presentation spells it out pretty clearly. Apple's SOR—the way in which it could focus its best capabilities in order to avoid bankruptcy (discontinuity) and generate sustainable value for the market—was this:

DEFINE "NEW PRODUCT PARADIGMS" AND BUILD THOSE RESULTING PRODUCTS WITH THE "INCREDIBLY IMPORTANT MARKET SEGMENTS" FOR WHOM APPLE WAS "EXTRAORDINARILY RELEVANT" IN MIND.

In other words, "Think Different." Then build products that *are* appreciably different—in feeling, look, and function. And all the while, ground those differences in the factors that were already influencing their biggest fans and brand ambassadors, the ones who would ultimately spread the word. Apple's SOR was to make products that helped increasingly connected and accelerated "global citizens" to navigate their exponentially changing world with greater ease and simplicity.

So what were the conditions that revealed this blueprint of possibility to Apple? If a SOR is a constellation, can we pick out the individual stars that gave it its footprint?

Technological Conditions

First and most obviously, Apple perceived the critical importance of technological developments in their mega-sphere of conditions. In the mid-nineties, broadband and wireless Internet was becoming faster and more robust, increasingly able to handle larger loads of data. Since according to Moore's Law increases in speed and strength are exponential, it made sense to try to build products that would meet the needs of customers in the near future.

Soon, the demand for devices that would give people new and better ways to tap into this ever-increasing flow of information would be red hot. People were already starting to embrace multi-smart devices. The popularity of phones that incorporated features like cameras and easy access to email and text proved that people were hungry for mobile computing. Consumers clearly wanted to have the power of the Internet "at hand".

Apple needed to be the first company to meet that demand in a game-changing way. Indeed, they would act in such a timely manner that consumers didn't have enough time to realize they even felt the need before it was already fulfilled. Apple's rollout of products acted like a row of dominoes, toppling demand with supply in an elegant proprietary row. A device like the iPod enabled unprecedented data storage, which then sparked a demand for data supply... and so the iTunes platform was born to accommodate that demand. The iPhone enabled unprecedented mobile computing power, which sparked a demand for novel applications...and so the App Store was born to accommodate that demand. Apple anticipated the way technology would influence demand and they simply built new business models to fit that emergent demand.

Furthermore, these products were designed to look good and be as simple and user-friendly as possible. Even though they were born out of exponentially accelerating technological changes, the products didn't feel bewildering or foreign. They gave us technology that made the complex appear simple. They made participating in disruptive times feel easy, natural and cool.

That's how Apple "invented" the future. Apple saw how emergent conditions were shaping up, and choose to stay a few steps ahead of everybody else.

Social Conditions

Apple also understood the human condition. They knew how to leverage the intense brand loyalty they commanded, and how it factored into a larger context of increasing "tech consciousness."

By 1997, the "Mac versus PC" argument was commonplace, with either side happy to passionately argue the virtues of their chosen OS. The rivalry between Microsoft and Apple was legendary. Macintosh computers had long ago established a reputation for ease of function and reliability, and in Jobs' 1997 Macworld address, he correctly identified Apple as being one of the world's top five best-loved brands. The "Think Different" campaign would never have caught on if it hadn't tapped into a passion for what Apple products represented to its fans. If they could just deliver on that brand promise of changing the world through empowering smart people to do more with technology, they believed their fans could create a groundswell of demand for Apple products.

But beyond Apple fandom, there was a growing feeling in the broader culture of needing to keep up with the pace of technology in order to keep up with the Joneses. The Blackberry phone had suddenly become the signifier of high-status business people everywhere. Owning one meant you were plugged into the times and not just in a cultural sense. A Blackberry gave you access not only to information, but also to a fast-growing array of transactional capabilities that connected you in real-time to a globalized world.

Apple perceived tremendous opportunity within social conditions—namely, the need for status and attachment to brand—in the mid-nineties. It's not difficult to see how these conditions continue to define the Apple strategy to this day.

Micro-Conditions

Remember Buzz Holling's adaptive cycle? This cycle, based on what Holling observed about how ecologies develop, envisions change moving in two directions: a forward loop of growth and conservation, and a backward loop of destruction and innovation. In other words, growth is good, but it doesn't happen through dogged conservation. Equally important is the growth that occurs when accumulated energy is released into innovation. This is when new life forms spring up. It's the wildfire that ultimately makes the forest a richer ecosystem. Release and re-think.

Jobs understood this perfectly. "Think Different" is nothing if not the clarion call of the backward loop. If Apple had persisted in just "making boxes for people to get their jobs done" it would have been holding on too tightly to that forward loop of legacy growth. This would have led Apple down the path of becoming a monotonous stand of trees, a perfect stack of tinder for a conflagration they would no longer be able to control or derive benefit from. If they decided in 1997 to just be more efficient at building better "boxes" then, they really might have suffered the same fate as Kodak. It would have been an easy mistake to make. After all, Jobs was correct when he said that they built those boxes "better than almost anybody in some cases." Holding onto a legacy like that—being "true" to what you do best—is a very common rationale for very poor strategies.

Jobs alluded to Apple's favorable micro-conditions during his Macworld Expo presentation when he praised the organization's "great" and "extraordinary" people. As he put it then, the "ability of the organization to execute is really high." He had the right people to pull off what he was envisioning. He saw that the micro-conditions within his organization were right for releasing and re-thinking Apple's enviable legacy. He also helped this along by cleaning house and ensuring the organization had a brand new Board, one that would champion his plan for radical innovation.

With these critical micro-conditions in place, Jobs and his people were able to ignite the controlled wildfires that ultimately renewed the Apple ecosystem.

HOW TO SEE AND SEIZE SORS—OR MISS THEM ENTIRELY

At this point, you might be inclined to remind us that hindsight is 20/20. After all, it's easy to glibly list what Apple got right and what Kodak got wrong as if the correct SORs in each case had been patently obvious to anybody with a brain. Of course, it's never that simple. But we believe there are a few ways you can prepare your organization to better perceive SORs when you look into conditions—and conversely, there are a few surefire ways to miss them.

How to Miss SORs

We've discussed the ways in which the traditional strategic planning process has failed to keep pace with the disruptive age. Conventional risk management is suffering a similar fate as those cycles of accelerating change roll on. The risk management model that too many leaders default to originates from an age when captains of industry were taught to preserve their vessels at any cost.

> **" *A PESSIMIST SEES THE DIFFICULTY IN EVERY OPPORTUNITY; AN OPTIMIST SEES THE OPPORTUNITY IN EVERY DIFFICULTY."***
>
> *Winston Churchill*

Nowadays, even with all of their industrious ship maintenance work, the captains are steering straight into M.A.D. Even in its final moments, just before the ship is dashed against the rocks, it is in brilliant condition, immaculately managed.

Traditional risk management teaches you to focus on just three capabilities: operational, reporting, and compliance.

This teaches organizations to be well run, with processes and workflows that provide for maximum efficiency. It also teaches the value of thorough and accurate reporting. And it stresses the importance of legal compliance. These are the marks any organization needs to hit to be considered a sound operation, a sea-worthy vessel.

This emphasis on efficiency, accuracy and stability was appropriate in the past, when the norm was long-term trends, incremental growth, and smooth sailing ahead. Organizations in this era experienced change in single digits. It made perfect sense to preserve a good thing once you found it. If it wasn't broke, you didn't fix it—you just streamlined it as much as you could. You could run a tight ship and expect to cruise toward a singular goal: "milking the cash cow".

But we know that this era is long gone. We live in disruptive times, which means we are experiencing accelerating and complex change. Enormous shifts are occurring in abbreviated cycles. This is double-digit change, exponential change, disruptive change. In this era, too strong an emphasis on operational efficiency can encourage legacy-lock-in and clinging to stranded assets. Kodak, for example, tried to manage its risks by doubling down on its efforts to become efficient. It "went lean", managed harder, and all the while insisted on pushing its stranded assets further down the throat of a market that had lost its taste for film-based photography.

PAUSE AND CONSIDER: *What does your organization's formal risk management process look like? Do you go beyond operational, reporting, and legal compliance?*

In disruptive times, we keenly feel what's missing from the traditional model of risk management. Beneath those three capabilities of conventional risk management exists a deeper capability, an even more elemental stratum that causes quakes when it shifts, crumbling the well-made structures we attempt to build atop it.

This stratum is the Strategic. It's our capability to manage strategic risk that ultimately determines whether we are positioned to generate sustainable value, or whether we've unknowingly built our city on top of the San Andreas Fault. Jobs indicated his sensitivity to this stratum when he assured his Macworld Expo audience that they had the right people, but they were laboring under the wrong strategy.

It's all too easy to lose touch with these strategic capabilities. Remember that hermetically sealed executive office? When there are a few of them in the same organization and they all keep their doors shut, you'll have problems.

Strategy people and risk management people tend to occupy strict silos, tucked away in their separate departments. They don't always get along or even seek each other out. Too often the risk department is seen as a poor cousin to the strategy department. The strategy people create plans meant to drive the organization forward but pay little heed to the inherent risks in the plan. If the strategy is successful, blissfully ignorant celebration ensues. But if the strategy unravels, it often appears on the risk register long after the damage is done and the value has been destroyed.

Strategic risk management and mitigation goes deeper than operational excellence, diligent reporting, and following the law to the nth degree. It's the wave a *united* organization has decided to steer directly into on the choppy waters of exponential change.

When you incorporate strategic risk assessment into your framework for risk management, you are prepared to ask more fundamental questions. You aren't content to ask yourself,

"Are we efficient?" You want to know, "Is our very existence sustainable given the conditions that are coming our way?" And you know your entire team is asking the same thing.

How to See SORs—and Seize Them

If persisting in traditional risk management models is a surefire way to miss the boat, then cultivating creativity within a sensible structure is the right way to sharpen your organizational strategy. But what do we mean by creativity, and how can we build structures that nurture and focus it?

> **" RISK COMES FROM NOT KNOWING WHAT YOU'RE DOING."**
> *Warren Buffett*

Let's turn, once again, to Mr. Jobs, who told *Wired* in 1995 that:

> *Creativity is just connecting things. When you ask creative people how they did something, they feel a little guilty because they didn't really do it. They just saw something.*
>
> *It seemed obvious to them after a while. That's because they were able to connect experiences they've had and synthesize new things. And the reason they were able to do that was that they've had more experiences or they have thought more about their experiences than other people.*
>
> *Unfortunately, that's too rare a commodity. A lot of people in our industry haven't had very diverse experiences. So they don't have enough dots to connect and they end up with very linear solutions without a broad perspective on the problem. The broader one's understanding of the human experience, the better design we will have.*

Creativity emerges in its most potent form from the collective creative consciousness of a diverse group. This is part of the reason why in Chapter 3 we advocated so strenuously for a diversity of sources and voices in any conditions assessment process. Remember your network of listening posts?

A greater breadth of knowledge and experience makes for richer cluster and pattern recognition and more dynamic solutions. In fact, the more dots, the more creative possibility. Creative people need enough dots to connect before they can produce anything that feels truly new. A diversity of experience makes for better design, and a diversity of perspectives makes for better SOR recognition.

PAUSE AND CONSIDER: *Can you think of an instance where something genuinely creative took place in your organization? How does your team demonstrate creativity?*

How do you take a diversity of experience, knowledge, and perspective and allow it to flow through a structure that provides focus and meaningful parameters? After all, not all SORs are created equal. After extolling the virtues of creativity, curiosity, and innovation, we need to pause and give common sense its due. You can't blunder headlong into any SOR and expect to reap a reward. An adventurous spirit is necessary for this journey, but so too is a roadmap.

Yes, there is such a thing as a definable structure that enables freeform creativity to flourish into something of value. Scoring SORs is our version of that structure.

It shouldn't be difficult to understand that SORs have varying levels of risk and opportunity. There are high risk and low opportunity SORs, low risk and high opportunity SORs, and every variation in between. Picture any given SOR as a dot on the following graph:

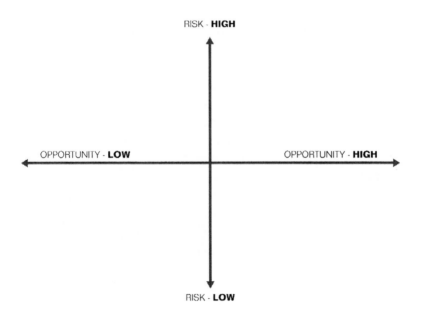

RISK - **HIGH**

OPPORTUNITY - **LOW**   OPPORTUNITY - **HIGH**

RISK - **LOW**

Diagram 4.1 | **THE HIGHS AND LOWS OF STRATEGIC OPPORTUNITY-RISK**

SORs have varying levels of risk and opportunity. There are high risk and low opportunity SORs, low risk and high opportunity SORs, and every variation in between.

If it's logical to highly rate "low risk, high opportunity" SORs, then SORs should also be prioritized in terms of just how "valuable" they are to your organization. Apple's creativity and the diversity of SORs that could have revealed themselves in those mid-nineties conditions had the potential to lead Jobs' team on a wild goose chase of freeform play. But Apple's innovations remained grounded in their well-established organizational values: to make powerful technological instruments that were pleasurable to use. They knew just what value they wanted to generate and it helped them to maintain focus.

ARBITRAGE: THE GOOD, THE BAD, AND THE M.A.D.

When you're deciding what constitutes a winning SOR for your organization, it's important to note that you can sometimes lay-off risks associated with an SOR. This is our interpretation of arbitrage, or as we like to call it, "entrepreneur's delight". This is where a seasoned player leverages opportunity-risk by taking on the risk they can cover but laying off a proportion of the risk to other parties. In return the entrepreneur shares the opportunity with the other parties commensurate with the risk those parties have taken. A perfect match of opportunity and risk between all parties is called "a good deal".

Apple, once again, furnishes us with a great example of arbitrage with its "iPlatform". iTunes and the App Store are mostly populated by content created by others. The iPhone and iPad are a blank canvas for apps created by developers who need to come through an Apple intermediary. These "content-creators" shoulder most of the risk when they make their music and their apps, while Apple takes on the (smaller) risk of providing a distribution platform. Even though Apple's share is small on a per transaction basis, it's still incredibly large when you consider how little of the overall risk they shoulder. This is brilliant arbitrage, and as you can see, it's more pleasant to be on Apple's side.

Having said this, arbitrage can backfire. For instance, when you view your conditions map you may identify instances where you are bearing the risk and the related opportunity is being enjoyed by another organisation. We call this unfair arbitrage.

Organizations on either side of these transactions risk falling into M.A.D. when they don't generate sustainable value. These relationships are one-sided and frequently unsustainable. Take for instance the ways in which large supermarket owners put undue risk onto small to medium suppliers. They make them provide stock on a "sale or return" basis, pay for promotions and prime in-store shelf-space, and wait for payment well outside of fair terms of trade. The opportunity enjoyed by the supermarket is completely out of balance with the suppliers' risk.

Suppliers within these arrangements find it very difficult (if not impossible) to gain and retain a healthy margin. In many cases these suppliers never generate sustainable value because the very process of building their businesses up to meet supermarket demands forces them into M.A.D. These arrangements are a surefire way to kill the very suppliers that feed these supermarkets. Everybody loses.

Enter into unfair arbitrage at your own risk.

PAUSE AND CONSIDER: *Are you currently falling prey to unfair arbitrage? Are you shouldering the risks while another party enjoys the opportunity? Or are you exposing yourself by crushing your suppliers under the risks you're laying off to them?*

HERE'S TO THE CRAZY ONES

The centerpiece of Apple's 1997 "Think Different" campaign was a television commercial that paired black and white images of 20th century icons with a voice-over by the actor Richard Dreyfuss, who read a short speech entitled "The Crazy Ones."

> **" IF THERE IS A SENSE OF REALITY, THERE MUST ALSO BE A SENSE OF POSSIBILITY."**
>
> *Robert Musil*

When it hit television screens, it was an instant smash. It spoke to people who saw innovation as a product of the human personality operating at peak capacity. They were ready to see Jobs and his engineers, coders, and designers as luminaries on the level of Albert Einstein and Pablo Picasso.

Most importantly, both old and new Apple fans alike wanted to see *themselves* as inventors, imaginers, healers, explorers, and creators. They believed that they themselves were the "crazy ones" who could "push the human race forward." They wanted to be active participants in a future that was unfolding before them at an exponential rate.

ARE YOU WITH THEM? IF SO, WHAT ARE YOU GOING TO DO ABOUT IT?

Disruption Readiness Checklist #2

☐ We know that any given Strategic Opportunity Risk is revealed in conditions and embodies both a certain level of risk and a certain level of opportunity.

☐ We know that a SOR exists to shine a light on how we might take active steps to generate sustainable value while managing and mitigating strategic risks.

☐ We know that we'll miss SORs or fall foul of disruptive change if we stick to a risk management model that strictly focuses on operational, reporting, and compliance capabilities and fails to sufficiently address strategic risk.

☐ We know we'll identify SORs if we cultivate creativity in our team and focus that creativity within a structure that scores SORs and helps us activate the best ones for generating sustainable value, managing and mitigating strategic risk, and avoiding unfair arbitrage.

CHAPTER 5

The Bottom-Line & Beyond

GENERATING SUSTAINABLE VALUE

HOW TO MOVE TOWARDS GENERATING SUSTAINABLE VALUE WITHIN THE SIA ALGORITHM, AND HOW WHOLE FOODS CREATED A WINNING STRATEGY OUT OF AN ENHANCED UNDERSTANDING OF WHAT VALUE IS AND HOW IT WORKS WITHIN INTERDEPENDENT NETWORKS.

" I BELIEVE OUR PHILOSOPHY OF CONSCIOUS CAPITALISM WILL EVENTUALLY BE WIDELY ADOPTED PRIMARILY BECAUSE IT IS A BETTER WAY TO DO BUSINESS, AND IT CREATES MORE TOTAL VALUE IN THE WORLD FOR ALL OF ITS STAKEHOLDERS."

John Mackey

THE UNHOLY MARKET

I n 1978, the people of Austin, Texas, didn't quite take to the new grocery store John Mackey opened up in his garage for them.

SaferWay Natural Foods was an enterprise after Mackey's own idealistic heart. Its offerings were strictly vegetarian, and devoid of sugar, caffeine, or alcohol. If Mackey didn't eat it, then he wouldn't sell it. His suppliers were Texan hippies and local farmers, and his partner was Renee Lawson, his fellow college dropout girlfriend. Mackey had been studying philosophy and religion at the University of Texas at Austin, but he found himself wanting to launch a retail career. He was a newly minted entrepreneur, ready to serve a market niche he believed had potential.

After the first year, half of the $45,000 USD Mackey and Lawson raised had evaporated. It was time for a re-think.

Mackey and Lawson decided to merge with another health food outfit, Clarksville Natural Grocery, and move to a larger location. They adopted a new name and a new strategy. The newly christened Whole Foods Market would define its parameters a little differently than SaferWay had. Instead of reflecting Mackey's personal preferences to the extreme, Whole Foods would offer the products people clearly wanted to buy—but with a difference. They would sell desserts, meat, convenience foods, and more, but all of it would be organic, preservative-free, and sourced from more ethical suppliers. They made a conscious choice not to be "Holy Foods Market," as Mackey puts it. Instead, they were going to introduce organic food to mainstream America, served up sans radical hippie judgment.

In 2014, Whole Foods was marking a successful rebound from the 21st Century's take on the Great Depression with four consecutive years of growth. That year, its revenues had increased by 10% to reach $14.2 Billion. It was a year of expansion, with 1,000 new locations in smaller urban centers like Boise, Idaho, and Detroit, Michigan. Reaching out to these markets was a bold move for the outfit that had earned the nickname "Whole Paycheck" for its pricey, upscale offerings and yuppie clientele. But if Whole Foods was going to make good on its mission to bring organic, values-conscious food to the mainstream, it was clear where they had to be. Middle America was waiting.

To make it work, they modified their approach. Low-income locations were stocked with more value brands and lower-priced items. They customized the Detroit store so that it felt more "Rock City" than "Left Coast", building food court tables out of car scraps and hanging Motown records from the ceiling. Defying expectations, the Detroit Whole Foods—along with other unlikely new locations—brought in the customers. They wanted what was on offer.

Whole Foods is famous for operating in accordance with "seven core values." These values run the gamut from "We create wealth through profits and grow" to "We practice environmental stewardship." Taken together, these seven values paint a picture of an enterprise commanding a unique space in American commerce. Capitalistic, yet values-based. Intent on capturing market share, yet operating under specific voluntary constraints. A lifestyle tastemaker grounded in market demand. Its seven core values tell the story of a company attempting to serve an unusually broad array of stakeholders: employees, suppliers, customers, investors, and the natural environment itself.

In 2004, John Mackey explained it to *Grist* like this: "I think one of the most misunderstood things about business in America is that people are either doing things for altruistic reasons or they are greedy and selfish, just after profit. That type of dichotomy portrays a false image of business. It certainly is a false image of Whole Foods. The whole idea is to do both: the animals have to flourish, but in such a way that it'll be cheap enough for the customers to buy it."

VALUE, AT THE CENTER OF IT ALL

Here, in the middle of this book, and in the center of the SiA algorithm, we arrive at value. And that's appropriate. After all, value is at the center of it all. Generating sustainable value is *the* purpose. It's our true north and *raison d'etre*. Value is expressed in measurable and hardnosed outputs—a healthy paycheck or a fat bottom line—as well as in less tangible, more *felt* and *experienced* manifestations. A culture shift, a new *zeitgeist*. Rock City patrons noshing on farm-to-plate edibles on the reclaimed parts of classic cars.

Without value, why bother? Without value, nobody cares. You may as well be a wild prophet of garage-based grocers, bleeding your investors dry.

In a sense, it's easy to define value. It's whatever needs to be there in order for anybody to care. Defining how you generate value—that most essential rite of organizations that go forth and remain solvent—mostly boils down to answering that very simple question: why would anybody care about us?

PAUSE AND CONSIDER: *When you ask yourself why anyone would care about your organization, what's the very first thing that pops up in your mind?*

But sometimes answering the simplest question adequately involves the subtlest thinking. It can involve the kind of lateral leaps that allowed Mackey to become a most unlikely capitalist hero. Mackey built the Whole Foods brand on a value proposition—organics for the mainstream—that takes the chain in unexpected directions as it unfolds. The way Whole Foods has chosen to define and deliver value has earned it legions of fans, but it's also secured a healthy contingent of detractors. Whole Foods has been a target of People for the Ethical Treatment of Animals and other protesters for its sale of meat products and its mainstream chain mentality. Groups like the Organic Consumers' Association call out the libertarian Mackey for his "dumb, hypocritical, conservative" views.

But the bottom line is Whole Foods' bottom line—and how a complement of seemingly non-financial concerns appears to feed into its thriving profit margins. And indeed they are thriving. Mackey's Unholy Food Market is dominant in a market that is growing every year. Whole Foods secures higher returns on capital investments than its competitors in the food retail industry. They sell more food per square foot than other mainstream grocery chains. They are winning.

Mackey's brand of idealism appears here to stay, at least for the foreseeable future.

So, here, at the center of it all, before we examine the place of value in the SiA algorithm, it might serve us to understand how someone like Mackey defines value. How does an empire-builder like Mackey decide how and to whom he should deliver value? Who are Whole Foods' various stakeholders— and can they really all get along? The way Mackey answered these questions meant the difference between a failed passion project and a niche-dominating juggernaut. The way *you* answer them could mean the difference between a disrupted organization and a state of continuous prosperity and purpose.

DEFINING VALUE

From its place as the centre-point of the SiA algorithm, to its place at the heart of any thriving venture, value is a concept that cries out to be investigated more deeply. Leaders and teams with the ability to steer towards continuity in times of disruptive change have learned to think bigger when it comes to value. Armed with this deeper thinking, they are able to guide their organizations towards ongoing prosperity and purposefulness. Let's try to catch up with them by conducting our own investigation.

Value in Basic Terms

Value, in its most essential form, is anything of importance, worth, or usefulness. And for the most part, we're talking about the measurable and the monetary when we talk about value. Value is $9.99 for a bag of widgets. Value, to paraphrase Warren Buffet, is whatever they will pay you for it.

Say you were asked to write up a list of discrete

> **" WHAT IS A CYNIC? IT IS A MAN WHO KNOWS THE PRICE OF EVERYTHING AND THE VALUE OF NOTHING."**
>
> *Oscar Wilde*

items, both tangible and intangible, that might have some measurable value within your organization. What would that laundry list of value look like? You might jot down: capital, environmental resources, the capacity to value-add, processes, contracts, networks, human resources, intellectual property, brand power, and products and services. Did we miss anything?

PAUSE AND CONSIDER: *What if you actually did take the time to create this list? What would be on your organization's priorities for value?*

Now imagine you arranged these discrete units of value into an equation that represented all of them coming together to generate something bigger, a kind of synergistic output of value. It might look like this:

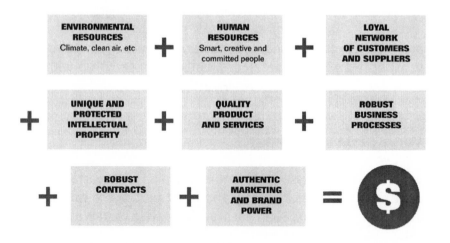

Diagram 5.1 | **THE SIA VALUE EQUATION**

Financial gain is a real but relatively small input and output in the SiA value equation. There are a diversity of factors that need to be valued before realizing sustainable financial gain.

The bottom-line is that no matter how you stack the value equation, financial gain is not created in isolation. Money never made money without the value equation in place.

Seems straightforward enough. So the question remains: is financial gain your *only* valued output? Or is it just one output of an even greater network of value? Is your organization stuck on measuring its value in strictly financial terms, and is that sustainable? Or is your value equation your means of measuring the breadth and depth of the value you deliver to customers and capture for your own organization?

Remember where the focus on financial thinking got Kodak. In the late nineties their stock prices had never been higher. Myopic calculations will only get you so far. We have to go beyond the basics.

Value and Your Business Model

Value generation—the ability to deliver and capture value—is the core of any business model. The delivery of value to external parties (eg. customers and suppliers) and the capture of value for internal parties (eg. employees and shareholders) should be at the heart of any business model. As Saul Kaplan explains in his book *The Business Model Innovation Factory*: "A business model is a story about how an organization creates, delivers, and captures value".

A business model is only ever sound when it honors the First Principle. When you have a good grip on conditions, identify the right SORs, develop the capability to deliver, and launch catalytic actions that provide the best bang for buck, you naturally generate value. And if you don't, your business model is shot.

We personally enjoy the way Kaplan describes a business model that fails due to disintermediation as being "netflixed". In his book he provides a list of well-known organizations that have either been, or are in the process of being, *netflixed*. Apart from the obvious titular example, Kaplan lists Amazon *netflixing* Borders, email *netflixing* postal services, online education *netflixing* universities, and Craigslist *netflixing* local newspapers. We could add: alternative energy supplies and domestic battery storage *netflixing* fossil fuel energy generators, electric vehicles *netflxing* fossil fuel powered vehicles, and driverless cars *netflixing* Uber (yes, even the grand disruptors need to beware).

Kaplan wrote his book in 2012, so in it he refers to the possibility of Netflix itself being *netflixed*. At that time, the Netflix business model relied on the value generated by its DVD rentals. Kaplan anticipated the potential for future disruption when he said: "Of course the biggest disruption to Netflix's business model comes from the ability to download or watch movies directly online". Fortunately for Netflix, since 2012 it exponentially shifted its business model to firmly position itself as a market leader in the online video business. And now it's in the process of *netflixing* the cable television business model. Netflixing averted.

The ongoing success of any business model is never guaranteed. And it's certainly never a right. Value generation is a privilege afforded to an organization by the conditions of the day. In the era of disruption, the business model use-by date for many organizations is already stamped on the packet. And in some cases, that date has come and gone.

As George Harrison says, "All things must pass."

PAUSE AND CONSIDER: *What is the use-by date for your current business model? It is looming? Has it passed?*

Value in Terms of Networks

Here's the thing. Have you ever taken the time to observe a dollar bill sitting on a countertop? It doesn't do much, does it? Sure, the value of that dollar bill is right there, printed explicitly on both sides of the note, but it's not really worth anything stranded on the countertop. However, as soon as it finds its way into the billfold of a human being, its value has the potential to be expressed and even multiplied. It could secure a candy bar or become part of a stock portfolio. That dollar bill needs to be transacted within a *value network* to count for anything at all.

Those who think in terms of broader organizational systems know how "value partners" come together to create reciprocal networks of value generation. In these networks, that relatively simple unit of value—the dollar bill—becomes something different or greater as it passes through each stage of the transaction. It might start out being invested in a widget. Then each partner in the network gets a turn to value-add, or contribute another layer of value to that widget before passing it on.

At each stage of that transaction the *value equation* is the driver of all outputs.

If at any stage in this process a value partner ceases to value-add, they may fall prey to disintermediation. In other words, they become a middleman who gets unceremoniously *netflixed.* Can you recall the days when you used to stroll around a video store, selecting that evening's entertainment? Blockbuster is a terrific example of a company that wouldn't budge from delivering value in one format, and suffered the consequences of disintermediation. With the advent of online streaming, movie lovers were quite capable of satisfying their cinematic needs without incurring the expense and inconvenience of a Blockbuster visit.

But the most unbelievable twist in the Blockbuster story occurred in the year 2000. That year, it had the opportunity to purchase Netflix for $50 Million USD and took a pass. Fifteen years later, Netflix's market capitalization was close to $35 Billion USD (higher than CBS), and Blockbuster was filing for bankruptcy protection.

It's a M.A.D. world.

Value in Terms of Interdependence

" FOR SOMETHING TO COLLAPSE, NOT ALL SYSTEMS HAVE TO SHUT DOWN. IN MOST CASES, JUST ONE SYSTEM IS ENOUGH. FOR EXAMPLE, THE HUMAN BODY IS A SYSTEM OF SYSTEMS. IF JUST ONE SYSTEM, SUCH AS THE CARDIOVASCULAR SYSTEM, SHUTS DOWN, DEATH FOLLOWS."

Robert Kiyosaki

When he thinks back on those initial stakeholder meetings, Fred Presley can clearly remember the skepticism.

As a planner for the Rhode Island Department of Environmental Management, he was involved in a project overseen by Kip Bergstrom of the Rhode Island Economic Policy Council and facilitated by Larry. The project bought people together to get them to talk about the Rhode Island watersheds, bays, and coastal areas. At the time, in the early 2000s, the shoreline of Narragansett Bay was in many parts an industrial wasteland. The group of about thirty people who gathered to discuss what needed to be done were by no means on the same page. Developers, engineers, architects and investors mixed uneasily with environmental advocates, government staff and non-profit folks. The idea was to get the group talking in the same language—to talk SiA. Initially they weren't buying it. Conditions? Networks? Interdependence? *Bah.*

"Everybody came in with their own agenda," explains Presley. "And each agenda had value in its own niche. But the niches weren't talking to each other very well."

The environmental groups argued vociferously for wetland restoration and wetland restoration *only*. Operating under the assumption that urban development and environmental restoration initiatives were mutually exclusive, they regarded development talk suspiciously.

But eventually the skepticism eased. The face-to-face encounter "forced a shift in perspective," as Presley recalls. The environmental advocates were aligning with the development community on how the right projects could enhance the coastal environment—and how environmental restoration *had* to become part of the equation if certain projects were to take off. Nobody, for example, would stay at a hotel on a ruined beach. Suddenly, these disparate stakeholders were able to talk, and beyond that to *plan* together. They realized that's exactly what they had to do if either group was going to produce anything of value.

Just as we are often blind to the conditions that aren't right in our face, demanding our time and attention in the micro-sphere, we can also overlook the multitude of connections that constitutes our networks of value. These are the networks we—knowingly and unknowingly—depend upon in order to generate anything worth anything. Sure, we're aware of the first few layers in this network—say, our buyers and suppliers—but beyond that, we usually aren't looking.

Here's a quick question: when we talked about value partners coming together to create reciprocal networks of value, what came to your mind? Did you construct a simple model that included your organization, your customers, your suppliers, and little else?

Rhode Island's environmental advocates, government staff and commercial developers had little idea just how much interdependency and alignment existed between their respective values before they hashed it out, face to face. That's what unexpected interdependence looks like. And our unmapped networks of value are full of connections like theirs.

PAUSE AND CONSIDER: *Can you think of an organization you tend to be at odds with who might actually be your partner in an unexpected interdependent value network?*

Along with its seven core values, Whole Foods operates under a "Declaration of Interdependence", which reads: "Whole Foods Market is a dynamic leader in the quality food business. We are a mission-driven company that aims to set the standards of excellence for food retailers. We are building a business in which high standards permeate all aspects of our company. Quality is a state of mind at Whole Foods Market."

Now, what does this statement mean in terms of the need for Whole Foods to generate sustainable value for internal and external stakeholders? Why is this a statement of "interdependence"?

Mackey likes to talk about the importance of cultivating one's "systems intelligence." To illustrate the point, he describes a group of medical students studying gross anatomy by dissecting a human body. The students learn about the body's musculature, circulatory system, and major organs. It's all right there on the table. But, asserts Mackey, if this was all the students were exposed to, they would never really understand the body. They wouldn't understand health. To learn that, they would need to observe a living body interacting with its environment and ingesting various foods. Understanding the body involves learning about relationships. It involves learning about the connections between elements in a larger system. A *whole* system.

When we review the core values that feed into Whole Food's value proposition of "organics for the masses", we see their systems intelligence at work. We see that a wide variety of relationships have been accounted for. Each connection has its place in terms of a broad network of sustainable value generation. To wit, the seven values are:

- We sell the highest quality natural and organic products available.
- We satisfy, delight, and nourish our customers.
- We support team member excellence and happiness.
- We create wealth through profits and growth.

- We serve and support our local and global economies.
- We practice and advance environmental stewardship.
- We create ongoing win-win partnerships with our suppliers.
- We promote the health of our stakeholders through healthy eating education.

The usual suspects are all represented. Customers, suppliers, and shareholders are given their due. Profits matter. "Long-term shareholder value" matters. But the core values also give special consideration to the well being of employees, who work within "self-directed teams," and under salary caps that limit the compensation of any individual to nineteen times the average total compensation of all full-time employees. The "environmental stewardship" value is expressed through initiatives like an in-house "Responsibly Grown" rating system for the produce and flowers they sell. And, of course, the core values include a pledge to support the "greater production of organically and bio-dynamically grown food."

Whole Foods drive to generate sustainable value emerges at the point where all of these diverse stakeholders converge. Whole Foods is "America's healthiest grocery store", where "value is connected to values", meaning the retailer is committed to staking out a space where they can offer socially conscious products as cheaply as possible to as many demographics as possible. The goal is to become "America's healthiest grocery store," not the healthiest grocery store in Mackey's Austin garage. Protecting the many relationships represented by their list of core values is all part of generating sustainable value.

Increasingly, Whole Foods has plenty of company when it comes to accounting for all the seemingly "non-financial" connections that constitute a real value network. Take, for example, the trend toward integrated reporting. Integrated reporting shows companies how they are producing value over the short, medium, and long term by taking into account factors such as governance, strategy, and future prospects. It's an assessment of an organization's performance—and capacity for continuity—that involves more than just studying the bottom line.

Charles Nichols, a group controller at Unilever, explains his company's decision to adopt the integrated reporting process like this:

> *We live in a very volatile world, where businesses such as Unilever face issues that need long-term solutions...I see it as inevitable over time that non-financial information will become an ever more important part of our corporate narrative.*

> *There are enough highly publicized examples where companies have destroyed inordinate amounts of value because investors, and in some cases the boards, haven't really understood the business model and been able to ask the right questions at the right time.*

It seems as though Unilever's people are well aware that they are operating in exponential times, and they're fashioning a new "corporate narrative" in response. They also clearly understand that a "business model" is simply a process for delivering and capturing value. What examples come to your mind when you think about companies that have "destroyed inordinate amounts of value" because they didn't "ask the right questions at the right time"?

PAUSE AND CONSIDER: *What "non-financial" factors are part of your organization's business model? Have you thought about them lately? Have you acted on them lately?*

In Terms of SiA

Finally, we return to the SiA algorithm. Take another look at it. "Generating Value" is, of course, right where it belongs: at the centre.

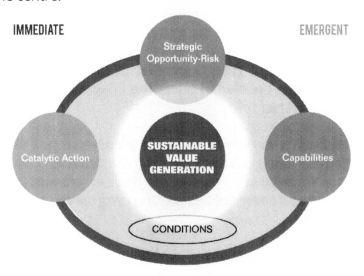

Diagram 5.2 | **VALUE GENERATION AND THE SIA**

Generating sustainable value is at the centre of the SiA Algorithm.

Since every organization exists to generate sustainable value for its external and internal stakeholders, it makes sense that value is front and center in the SiA framework. Value is generated out of the Strategic Opportunity-Risks that appear within conditions. Since SORs are double-sided coins, some organizations can experience value generation, and others value destruction, within the same conditions.

As always, it all falls apart without adherence to the First Principle. If the value your organization is trying to generate is not aligned with immediate and emergent conditions, then you're aiming for an SOR that has already evaporated. Good luck finding any return on that investment. Misalignment means value destruction. Once you stop generating value for yourself or your stakeholders, it's time to check state and see where you've fallen out of alignment.

PAUSE AND CONSIDER: *What would "value destruction" feel like in your organization? What would be a sign that you've somehow stopped generating sustainable value? Can you think of signs beyond "lagging sales" or "shrinking profit margins"?*

We are all focused on generating sustainable value. That means delivering value to external stakeholders like customers and suppliers, as well as capturing value for internal stakeholders like employees and investors within a whole and interdependent system. It means delivering it without interruption, without disintegration, and even in the midst of disruptive change. Value is our endgame.

Now...how do we play?

DEFINING YOUR ORGANIZATION'S OPPORTUNITY TO GENERATE SUSTAINABLE VALUE

" *WHENEVER I'VE HAD TO MAKE A MAJOR DECISION AS A DOCTOR, COP OR FOR A COMPANY I'VE WORKED FOR, I ASK MYSELF: WHAT IS THE VALUE PROPOSITION HERE? WILL MY DECISION BRING ADDED VALUE TO THE POPULATION I HAVE THE PRIVILEGE TO SERVE?"*

Richard Carmona

Equipped with a fuller sense of what value is and how value networks operate, are you now able to define the value your organization must generate in order to maintain continuity or leverage disruption in exponential times? Can you say what matters, and to whom? Can you say exactly what sustainable value you can expect to deliver and what value your organization will capture for itself?

Defining that value means answering these questions based on the solid intel you glean from assessing your conditions and associated SORs. It's all part of becoming a Dr. Reality. A true value proposition isn't an aspirational statement born out of corporate navel-gazing or a baseless vision. It isn't a feel good platitude or a marketing message—although good value propositions can function as such. Whole Foods' seven values might strike the cynical as simply empty brand-speak, but they are, in fact, descriptive of the company's actual strategic approach.

Defining the sustainable value you intend to generate requires a realistic and authentic assessment of what your organization can *truly* do. How can you proceed?

First, Validate Value in Your SORs

Remember the First Principle: *to generate sustainable value, opportunity-risk, capabilities and actions must continuously align with and within conditions.*

Without validating SORs to ensure they will generate sustainable value, all is for naught. As SORs reveal themselves like constellations in the starry skies of conditions, remember that any SOR is only worth as much as the value it will allow your organization to generate on a sustainable basis.

Next, identify both the possibilities for authentic value generation and the interdependent value networks that will make that value generation a reality.

Notice how they require and encompass so much more than just simple, financial outcomes. For example, your conditions might reveal an opportunity to grow and bond with a new customer network. That's a value that might resist easy quantification. But isn't it a SOR worth investigating? Especially if it develops capabilities that may strengthen your organization over the long run?

When thinking this through, keep Kodak and Blockbuster in mind. Which value networks and opportunities for long-term value generation did they ignore?

As you look into conditions and associated SORs, consider just a few of the markers of value that may or may not be embodied within what your organization delivers to others or captures for itself:

1. **Value Network:** the access to and ownership of customer and supplier networks that ensure a robust exchange and sharing of value (eg. Apple)

2. **Agility:** the knowledge, insight, creativity, commitment, and decision-making that allows for timely releasing, re-thinking and reorganizing in sync with changing conditions

3. **Conditions:** the intelligence at all scales enabling the identification of immediate and emergent conditions that are, will, or may impact the organization, *and* the ability to create a shared understanding of those conditions to support informed and timely decision-making

4. **Value-Adding Capability:** the ability to add value above and beyond industry or sector standard through the continual development of valued products, services and processes that differentiate you from your competition

5. **Environment:** the available natural resources, especially those that support your ongoing value generation (eg. clean air and water, stable climate, healthy soil, sustainable raw materials, secure sources of food, etc.)

6. **Financial:** the access to capital and potential for delivering an appropriate and sustainable return on investment

Mapping Out Value and Value Networks

Next, you must map out the critical nodes in your value network. Who are your partners in generating value? Do you have unexpected interdependencies? Who are the essential players and what value do they add to your value?

PAUSE AND CONSIDER: *Who would you miss if they suddenly disappeared from your organization's value network?*

It's ok to start simple. Begin with your customers and suppliers. But then look further. Who are your less obvious stakeholders?

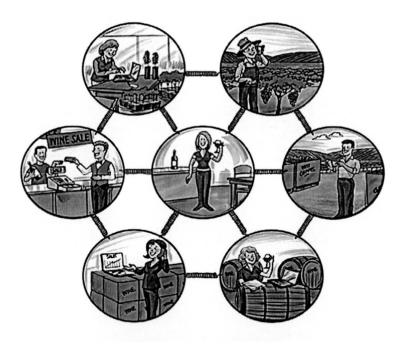

Diagram 5.3 | **A SIMPLE VALUE NETWORK**

When you map out your value network you may start with an illustration like this example from the wine industry. There are seven key value partners that all share interdependencies. If one fails, they are all impacted. In a more complex map other value partners could also be factored in such as energy providers, transport and media.

Now you should start to see your organization as a node in a web of reciprocal value generation. Whose problems are you solving? Who is solving your problems? How are you capturing value from this network, and how are you delivering value to it? And how long can this flow of value last? Is there anything in that network that threatens to impede or redirect this flow of value?

Finally, Put it Into Words

You've observed conditions and SORs. You looked for all sorts of value, from the immediate and easily quantifiable elements to the less tangible (but still critically important) factors. You've put your systems intelligence to the test and moved beyond corporate "gross anatomy" in order to see your organization as part of an interdependent network of relationships.

You mapped it out. Now, it's time to spell it out.

Define the sustainable value you are proposing to generate by answering the following questions:

1. What value will we deliver, and to whom?
2. What value will we capture, and from whom?
3. How will we measure the value generated (that is, captured and delivered)?
4. Is my entire team engaged, aligned, and committed to this value generation?

It need not be more complicated than this. Think about Whole Foods seven core values. Each, in its own way, is an answer to one of the above questions. And that's why it's a platform for a powerful value proposition. It's a proposition that, so far, has kept Whole Foods's customers, suppliers, shareholders, and employees in a relatively stable alignment. It feeds into messaging potent enough to spearhead a new movement towards what marketers are calling "conscious capitalism." Though Whole Foods' detractors rue the day Mackey decided he wasn't running a Holy Foods Market, so far nobody could accuse him of launching an enterprise that lacked staying power or influence. Whole Foods generates sustainable value, period.

BE AUTHENTIC

There's just one more thing you should consider if you intend to generate sustainable value out of the SORs your conditions reveal.

" TRUTH IS A POINT OF VIEW, BUT AUTHENTICITY CAN'T BE FAKED."
Peter Guber

You've got to deliver. The promises you make are crucially important. That's why you take the time to figure out how you factor into an interdependent network.

Authenticity matters. If your value proposition—and the branding that flows from it—rings hollow, your network will notice. And it will hurt you in the long run. The world is littered with large "looking good, going nowhere" organizations that were disintermediated by up-and-comers. Remember Netflix and Blockbuster.

In many ways, marketers have created an epidemic of M.A.D. Organizations are locked into spin branding that provides the illusion of authentic value. Consider banks that wax eloquent about caring for their customers while they evict them from their homes. Consider fast-food brands that extol the virtues of a great food experience while they pour fuel on the obesity epidemic. Consider anti-aging products that promise the fountain of youth even as they harm consumers with dubious ingredients.

The thing is, as Abraham Lincoln once said: "You can fool all the people some of the time, and some of the people all the time, but you cannot fool all the people all the time." Since the advent of social media, the lived experience of consumers is counting for more and more. Splashy marketing campaigns that don't cohere with true brand *experience* can no longer clobber the consumer consciousness into submission.

Whole Foods customers have made Mackey's chain one of the most trusted companies in the world because their lived experience adds up to the brand promise. The *experience* of shopping at their favourite grocery store reinforces their loyalty. From the informative labelling to the happy employees, Whole Foods has given its fans reason to believe in the value it delivers. And these customers are happy to share that experience publicly, which counts for everything in the age of social media.

So be real. Be authentic. Because you'll eventually have to prove it when you make claims about who you are and what value you can generate. After you've answered the question "Who cares?" you'll have to answer an equally important question: "Will they *keep* caring?"

GET READY TO DO WHAT IT TAKES TO DELIVER ON YOUR PROMISE.

Disruption Readiness Checklist #3

☐ We can answer the question of why people care about what we're doing—and how long they might keep caring.

☐ We understand that generating both financial and non-financial value within an interdependent network will pave the way for our organization's continuity and allow us to leverage discontinuity.

☐ We generate sustainable and authentic value out of the SORs revealed through our conditions analysis.

☐ We understand that if we try to capture or deliver value that isn't validated by our conditions analysis, we are at a high risk of creating value destruction.

☐ We can define the value we are delivering and capturing, and map out how that value flows through our value network.

CHAPTER 6	The Right Stuff

CAPABILITIES FOR MAKING IT ALL COME TO LIFE

HOW A ROBUST SYSTEM OF CORE CAPABILITIES ALLOWS AN ORGANIZATION TO MAKE GOOD ON ITS PROMISE TO GENERATE VALUE, AND HOW THE ELECTRIC CAR COMPANY TESLA REALIZED ITS REVOLUTIONARY MISSION BY MAKING THE RIGHT INVESTMENTS AT JUST THE RIGHT TIME.

" *NEW TECHNOLOGY IS FREQUENTLY QUITE EXPENSIVE, AND IT COMES IN AT THE TOP. CELL PHONES USED TO BE $2,000 APIECE…AND YOU'VE GOT TO BE ABLE TO GET THAT MARKET SHARE AND GET THE VOLUMES UP TO PUSH IT DOWN. SO, IT'S WEIRD TO THINK THAT ELECTRIC CARS WOULD START AT THE CHEAPEST POSSIBLE THING."*

Marc Tarpenning

BANKROLLING A REVOLUTION

General Motors noticed it first.

Only "environmentalists and tech enthusiasts" were buying their EV1, the first mass-produced electric car in history. So in 2003, they pulled the plug on the EV1 program and started to reclaim the vehicles from their distressed owners. GM told the public that there just weren't enough buyers to justify the infrastructure needed to build and service electric vehicles. And then they had them all crushed.

But there was something about that small group of green-minded and tech-loving EV1 fans that struck Martin Heberhard and Marc Tarpenning. The two entrepreneurs had recently founded Tesla Motors with the goal of bringing the electric car back to life and becoming a clean technology leader. GM's analysis intrigued them. They discovered that the people who bought the EV1 tended to make around $250,000 a year. And that when Toyota launched the high-priced Prius hybrid it sold surprisingly well, cannibalizing sales for another model.

The *Lexus.*

So Tarpenning and Heberhard decided they were going to build a car for the rich. They realized saving money on gas and oil didn't motivate electric vehicle enthusiasts. Rather, these "environmentalists and tech enthusiasts" wanted to make a statement about their values with a car that also satisfied their desire for luxury and performance.

They had their strategy: Tesla would crack the automotive market from the top down. They would achieve the scale necessary to eventually reduce costs for the average buyer by leveraging the willingness of the rich to invest in a compelling statement car. Like Jobs' "incredibly important market segments", these wealthy environmentalists and tech enthusiasts had pockets deep enough to fund a revolution.

The strategy was clear. Could Tesla pull it off?

Their feasibility study with a group called AC Propulsion convinced them they could create the large-scale packs of high-energy, low-density batteries that would accommodate the high performance vehicle they envisioned. They knew other automakers secured car parts from contractors so they figured they wouldn't have to make everything from scratch. They found a manufacturer called Lotus who agreed to take on the job. They knew they wanted to replace as much mechanical complexity as possible with software, so they drew heavily from the high tech well, hiring the most innovative designers and engineers in Silicon Valley. Finally, they connected with a large number of venture capitalists, including a certain angel investor named Elon Musk, whose breakout company PayPal had recently secured him more than a little renown.

With the Tesla machine firing on all cylinders, they built the Roadster, a zippy, sleek beauty of a car. Its acceleration was punchy beyond any conventional vehicle, thrilling the high-octane sensibilities of the true sports car aficionado. The Tesla Roadster had torque and style. It was a straight-up sexy car.

During the Roadster's early days, Tesla let a well-heeled tester take it out for a spin, hoping the experience would convert him into an investor. Tarpenning remembers the phone ringing shortly afterward. It was the tester on the other end, sounding peeved. What was the problem?

The upset tester let Tarpenning have it: "What the hell did you do to my Porsche? I just spent a quarter of a million dollars on this thing, and it sucks now!"

Cha-*ching*.

THE MAN OF THE HOUR

" *AMERICA STILL HAS THE RIGHT STUFF TO THRIVE. WE STILL HAVE THE MOST CREATIVE, DIVERSE, INNOVATIVE CULTURE AND OPEN SOCIETY—IN A WORLD WHERE THE ABILITY TO IMAGINE AND GENERATE NEW IDEAS WITH SPEED AND TO IMPLEMENT THEM THROUGH GLOBAL COLLABORATION IS THE MOST IMPORTANT COMPETITIVE ADVANTAGE."*

Thomas Friedman

Imagine you're a ruggedly handsome hero who has been gazing flinty-eyed through your front room window for about an hour or so. You've been watching a storm fit for the summer cinema broiling in the sky, steadily approaching your hometown. A panicked voice on the radio is warning listeners about an impending disaster. People are running out their front doors and starting up their station wagons.

You've seen enough. You know what you have to do. (Something about intercepting the tornado with an advanced piece of technology of your own design? Or at the very least, gripping a romantic interest tightly at some critical juncture as the rains lash you mercilessly?) You turn away from the storm and behold your reflection in a hallway mirror.

You ask yourself: *"Have I got what it takes?"*

You've seen this movie, right? Chances are when you've faced personal and professional challenges you've even searched through the repository of your cultural memory for action movie stereotypes like these. (We all need to feel like supermen sometimes.) Anyway, we trot out the B-movie narrative for your consideration because it's a pretty good representation of what is occurring at this juncture in our journey to "thinking SiA."

Up until this point, you've been looking out, out, out—further than you may be accustomed to looking, straining your vision to perceive even murky and abstract developments in the mega-sphere. You've been gazing through your front room window, evolving a plan, putting a finger on exactly what it is you need to do and for whom. And then you pause from looking outward to look within. You are taking a moment to figure out if you've got the right stuff.

That's what capability is. The right stuff.

WHAT CAPABILITY IS AND ISN'T

What we're going tell you next may feel like déjà vu all over again. Do you remember when you mapped out your value network, trying to figure out where you had resources that connected you with other value partners, making you a vital player

> **" SOME PEOPLE, THROUGH LUCK AND SKILL, END UP WITH A LOT OF ASSETS. IF YOU'RE GOOD AT KICKING A BALL, WRITING SOFTWARE, INVESTING IN STOCKS, IT PAYS EXTREMELY WELL."**
>
> *Bill Gates*

in virtuous cycles of value generation? We said you could find value in things like the environment, processes, networks, and people. And now we're going to tell you that your *capabilities* tend to appear via the following eight properties:

1. The environment
2. Your people
3. Your networks
4. Your software
5. Your hardware
6. Your processes
7. Your raw inputs
8. Your value-added outputs

Yes, we know. There appears to be overlap between what is considered "value" and what is considered "capability." We can explain. But first, let's dig into the basic definition.

Fortunately, the meaning of "capability" is pretty straightforward. It's the ability to do something, plain and simple. It's a radio that plays music. But "capacity" is the amount, size, strength, or depth of a capability. When the volume knob is turned to crank up the music so that the entire neighborhood can hear we get a sense of the capacity of the radio's music playing capability. Finally, "competency" is the level of skill or finesse with which a capability can be executed. It's, say, the fitness of the radio to pick up signals and broadcast them clearly, without static or interference, so that everybody in the neighborhood can hear the pure tones of the pop song they are being unwillingly subjected to.

If you were to take this radio and add it to your list of "items of value", you might justify its addition to the list with a footnote that reads: "Because the neighborhood needs to hear great music. My neighborhood *values* music." (You might need to work on your stakeholder interview skills, but that's beside the point.) Now if you were to add that same radio to your list of "capabilities", your footnote under that item might read: "Because it plays music loudly and clearly enough for the whole neighborhood to hear it." The radio is valuable, but only if the dials are working and you know how to use them.

Value is about looking outward and capability is about looking inward. When we see the resources we possess through the lens of what our stakeholders want from us, we see value. When we look at many of those same resources through the lens of what we intend to do—how we intend to *deliver* the value our stakeholders want—we see capability. Capability is the life force of value.

PAUSE AND CONSIDER: *Do you have any value you're not sure how to deliver? Are you able to name the capability that might bring that value to life?*

Capability is whatever organizations invest their time, money, and resources into. Imagine our B-movie hero dropping to the floor to crank out a quick twenty push-ups to strengthen his lithe body. He is making an investment in his heroic capabilities.

Focused capability is the engine of value generation, and value generation is at the center of SiA. Generating the right value is what counts. So if organizations invest in the wrong capabilities, they risk losing not only their investments, but also potentially the opportunity to go forth in an undisrupted state. Imagine if our hero spent all of his time doing push ups and neglected his engineering studies? He'd look good clutching his romantic interest, but we'd never get a chance to see his epic CGI triumph of technology over nature. Fortunately, he's our ideal hero, so that means he spent *just* enough time on upper body conditioning, and *just* enough time testing his prototypes.

PAUSE AND CONSIDER: *Where does your organization invest the majority of its time, money, and resources? Why?*

All of the capabilities representing your fitness to deliver value come together to form a system of capability. In this network—just as in your value network—the way these capabilities *connect* to enhance one another matters. As much as the word "synergy" has been used and abused by some in the business community, it's still the name of the game. The integration of your capabilities *does* need to produce a combined effect that is greater than their separate values. If 1 + 1 only equals 2 in your organization, you will obviously be muscled out by the organization for whom that same 1 + 1 equals 3, or even 10.

Capability isn't cash. Cash is something that can be used to acquire or access capabilities, but in itself it only represents the propensity to create capability. The same goes for assets. They, like cash, are only of value if they can be leveraged to support and strengthen an organization's capability. Apple's billion-dollar cash reserves may give them credibility and security, but the cash alone doesn't invent watches, make iPhones, or deliver iTunes. It's Apple's capability that does all of that.

The assets that put Kodak in the top tier of business were not able to protect them from bankruptcy. The only thing that could have prevented their fall would have been the decision to use those assets to acquire or access the capability they needed to compete in a changing market.

In disruptive change, assets are usually illiquid and only possess value if someone is prepared to pay for them in the context of the conditions present at the time of sale. In a best-case scenario, an organization can spend its cash on innovations that represent change ahead of change. In a worst-case scenario, they can return whatever cash remains to its shareholders after they close up shop.

In bankruptcy, Kodak received little in return for its camera film business assets. Would-be purchasers had long ago read the conditions and written off Kodak's trove as stranded assets. Similarly, buyers heavily discounted the intellectual property on offer. Those "great ideas" would have been useful to Kodak if they had fully leveraged them in their halcyon days of corporate dominance. But by 2012, that ship had sailed.

The lesson here is that continuity—especially in these disruptive times—cannot subsist on cash or assets alone.

Instead, leveraging value from discontinuity requires a special range of capabilities. The capability out of which Blockbuster created value for years was old, tired, and unprepared for the discontinuity game played by Netflix. As Netflix evolved its business, it had fewer assets and less cash than Blockbuster, but it was able to leverage a relatively unique capability for delivering value over and above what Blockbuster could offer.

CAPABILITY WITHIN SIA

Let's revisit the SiA algorithm. So far we have assessed our conditions in order to identify the SORs that provide the potential for generating sustainable value. Take yet another look at the SiA model:

IMMEDIATE   EMERGENT

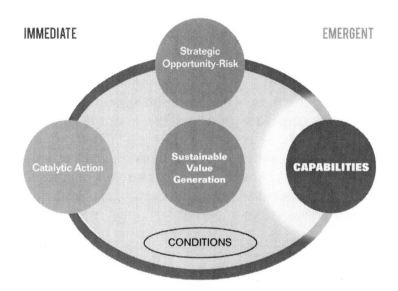

Diagram 6.1 | **CAPABILITY AND THE SIA ALGORITHM**

Capability – the ability to do something – is what organizations invest in to generate value. Identifying the right capabilities to invest in at the right time is what makes value generation sustainable.

In SiA, you learn to think about your capabilities after you have answered the question of how you can generate value. Thinking it through in that way allows you to better focus on what capabilities you need to access to generate that particular value. It's about looking at your organization through a lens that detects with finer resolution the capabilities you have, the capabilities you need to develop, and the capabilities you need to outsource in order to make good on your promise to generate the best, more enduring value possible.

In terms of generating that chosen value, not all capabilities are created equal. Some are obviously more relevant. If you can't focus on the critically important capabilities—or if you lack them entirely—the value you wanted to generate will remain a pipe dream. Your value proposition will fail, and that is a sure sign of going M.A.D.

It feels as if the more we explore the algorithm, the more self-evident the First Principle becomes. Alignment is everything. Although in practice, SiA is a fluid, interlocking sequence—a seamless way of thinking and acting—it really does make sense to learn it as a series of steps that build up to one very important outcome: providing the sustainable value that underpins your own continuity.

PAUSE AND CONSIDER: *Imagine you listed your organization's main capabilities without thinking of them in terms of their potential to generate sustainable value. Would that list look different from the one you might create within the SiA framework?*

Soon, we'll explore the tools you can use to *focus* your lens of value on the capabilities that matter. But first let's get a little more conversant with capabilities.

FROM THE GENERIC TO THE GAME-CHANGING

So now we've got the focus adjusted on our SiA thinking. We understand that capability is "the right stuff" for delivering the value we've determined we can generate based on our conditions and SORs. We know that sustainable value is our endgame and that not all capabilities are created

❝ OUR ENTIRE TEAM IS FOCUSED ON MANAGING THIS COMPANY FOR VALUE—FIXING OR ELIMINATING THOSE OPERATIONS THAT LESSEN VALUE AND EXPANDING OR ADDING THOSE THAT ENHANCE VALUE.❞

Phil Condit

equal. So how do we go about naming our capabilities, and placing them in a hierarchy of value-delivery? Let's explore a basic taxonomy of capability.

The General

This is the basic price of admission. General capabilities will get you to the door, but not quite over the threshold. They feature in just about every organization over a broad range of industries.

Let's imagine an airline that meets the general requirements for existing as an organization. It has HR, accounting, leadership, management, and marketing capability. It is a generic but operational outfit. It officially possesses the bare essentials for any organization to exist. We refer to these capabilities as "hygiene" capabilities.

The Specialized

Now we're getting somewhere. Specialized capabilities make you a marginal contender in your industry. They mean you have the abilities that are common to every organization in your specific industry or sector.

Our airline has the ability to fly, map its routes, maintain its aircraft, and ensure the safety of its customers. It's a basic airline company completely undifferentiated from any other airline in the world. It's Air Generic. Fly the friendly skies with Air Industry Standard.

The Value-Adding Over Industry or Sector Standard

This is where you start standing out, giving customers a reason to choose you over your competition. With value-added capabilities you rise above the industry standard.

You are delivering the unexpected.

Now our airline has business-class seats that convert into cozy sleeping chambers. We have flight attendants who tell jokes. We serve creative meals. We offer more legroom. Better entertainment choices. No longer Air Industry Standard, we have become Air Industry Leader.

PAUSE AND CONSIDER: *How difficult is it for you to quickly list some of your organization's general, specialized, and value-adding capabilities? Is it relatively easy to categorize them, or do you have some trouble figuring out whether some are "specialized, industry standard" or "value-adding over industry standard"?*

COMPETITIVE ADVANTAGE AT THE CORE

Your competitive advantage—defined as whatever helps you outperform your competitors—is the sum of your specialized and value-added capabilities. These capabilities exist in a core system that constitutes the real life force of your venture. It's the central nervous system without which an organization would be a completely different entity, geared to deliver a completely different variety of value.

> *IF YOU'RE TRYING TO CREATE A COMPANY, IT'S LIKE BAKING A CAKE. YOU HAVE TO HAVE ALL THE INGREDIENTS IN THE RIGHT PROPORTION."*
>
> *Elon Musk*

PAUSE AND CONSIDER: *How does the value your organization generates relate to your capabilities? Are these clearly value-adding or specialized capabilities?*

Since those early days of blowing back the hair of Porsche-owning test drivers, Tesla has been moving incrementally towards its goal of revolutionizing the automotive industry. Its newest product, the Model S, represents a step in the direction of producing those lower cost electric cars for the masses. It has been selling briskly and racking up awards for safety, performance, and environmental friendliness. And it boasts a very healthy share price indeed.

To fulfill their strategy, Tesla had to make all the right investments. Fortunately, it appears the founders knew just which pieces of the puzzle constituted a robust competitive advantage. They developed a precise system of core capabilities with the resources they possessed.

Most significantly, they leveraged the power of one of the Silicone Valley's finest minds: Elon Musk, who famously graduated from being Tesla's biggest investor to its CEO. Musk built his team as if they were the Special Forces of tech companies. He only allowed those who proved themselves to be of a certain caliber to remain, while the mere foot soldiers were sent packing.

These Tesla Special Forces focused their energies on cutting edge designs. They created cars that operated like computers, auto-updating like smartphones. They committed themselves to continually improving their battery technologies. Like Apple, they took control of distribution, building stores that complemented their brand with pleasurable and attractive environs. Finally, they created a ubiquitous network of Supercharger stations that allow Tesla drivers to power up their vehicles quickly and conveniently.

In other words, Tesla sank its teeth deeply into the capabilities that gave it a real edge in value adding over industry standard. They invested into *just* the right people and *just* the right technologies. Tesla had *focus*. Car parts weren't going to make or break them in the early days, so they could leave that piece to contractors like Lotus. Better battery technology, on the other hand, was the true game-changer. The right capabilities were organized around the right priorities, and a new industry leader was born.

A well-defined system of core capabilities does more than fulfill one-off strategies. It's what allows an organization to shape-shift when conditions change or new SORs appear on the horizon. In 2015, Tesla made headline news with Musk's announcement that the company would enter the energy market with a suite of low-cost solar batteries for homes, utilities, and businesses. It was an epic step forward in the struggle to achieve fossil fuel independence. It seemed Tesla's focus on improved battery technology and extraordinary design talent was enabling the company to make good on its value proposition in unexpected ways.

Hitting that value payload and launching a revolution in one fell swoop is a great outcome. In an ideal world, every organization would make perfectly timed investments, leveraging disruption with as much panache as Tesla Motors. But we don't live in that world, do we? So what happens when something clearly isn't working in an organization's capability mix?

CALIBRATING CAPABILITY

❝ *I HAVE ALWAYS TRIED TO LIVE BY THE PHILOSOPHY THAT WHEN THERE IS A BIG PROBLEM THAT NEEDS FIXING, YOU SHOULD RUN TOWARDS IT, RATHER THAN AWAY FROM IT.*❞

Henry Paulson

In the early 2000s, GM Holden was at a crossroads. The nineties had been good for the esteemed Australian automaker, but the new millennium brought with it a loss of domestic market share. By 2003, GMH surrendered the number one sales position in Australia to Toyota. The large sedans that Australian buyers had once been happy to snap up were giving way to more fuel-efficient models.

Still, Asia was an increasingly promising prospect. But breaking in there was proving tricky. An initial foray into the Korean market yielded frustration and not much else.

Holden's engineering strategist and Resilient Futures SiA practitioner Peter Vawdrey was charged with helping the company develop a strategy for becoming a real global contender. To do that, they had to solve the Asian puzzle. What was preventing Holden from making successful contact with customers? They knew what conditions were impacting them, and had a good handle on the risks and opportunities: environmental factors influencing Australian buying patterns, and economic growth driving demand in emerging markets. They also knew exactly where they wanted to go based on that assessment.

But it was time to shift from looking outward to looking inward.

Like many companies with a legacy of success, Holden didn't really examine what made them great until shifting conditions caused that greatness to come into question. Likewise, their inadequacies went undetected until the moment changes in their environment began to expose them to risk.

Why were they strong and how were they weak?

It was abundantly clear where Holden's strength lay. The automaker had great talent. Its team of designers and engineers were particularly efficient, capable of designing and engineering a range of high performance products to suit Australia's discriminating car culture. There weren't many engineering problems this team couldn't solve.

But Holden had a harder time solving certain non-technical puzzles. Specifically, they needed to improve communication—both within the organization and with external stakeholders. They just didn't understand the people they were trying to make products with, or the people they were trying to sell those products to.

Vawdrey explains it like this: "We were designing cars for drivers. But in Korea and China, you needed to design for the people sitting in the backseat."

He remembers a confused exchange between a Korean senior executive and the Holden engineers who were trying to understand why their decision to mount the air conditioning controls in the ceiling was unacceptable. From a functionality standpoint, it made good sense, didn't it? Finally, their Korean stakeholder managed to make his point.

"Look," he said, "the boss doesn't want to raise his arms!"

Ultimately, simple calibrations in the way Holden's team communicated made a big difference, paving the way for more successful incursions into the Asian market, and scoring the company big coups.

MEASURING AND MAPPING CAPABILITY

Maybe, like Tesla, you've nailed your competitive advantage by lining up all of the right ingredients in the right proportions. Or maybe, like Holden, you've had to make adjustments in order to continue riding the wave of disruptive change. Is there a way to gain clarity about where you're at, and how successfully you're focusing your capabilities to generate sustainable value?

We say there is. It's pretty straightforward. First, name your specialized and value-adding capabilities. Then measure the strength of each. Then look at each in the context of the network, asking yourself whether 1 + 1 is equaling 3 (or more) as often as it should.

To figure out exactly what an organization's core capability is, we use the SiA Capability Matrix, pictured below:

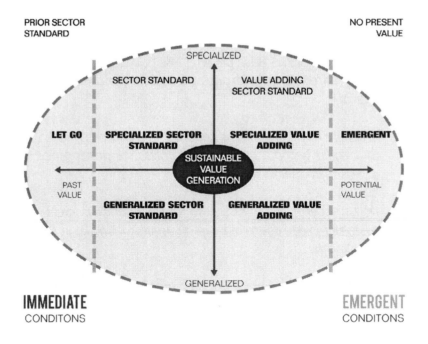

Diagram 6.2 | **THE SIA CAPABILITY MATRIX**
A tool to assist in the timely identification of, and investment in, the capability to maintain sustainable value generation.

This tool clarifies which capabilities keep us in the game, and which ones give us a competitive advantage that enables us to generate sustainable value.

It also allows us to keep "thinking SiA" by helping us to map out capabilities with respect to the immediate and emergent conditions impacting our organization and our industry.

The Matrix helps us to question:

> *Which capabilities mattered last year, and which ones will give us the cutting edge in the years to come by delivering authentic value over industry standard? (After all, last year's value-add always becomes this year's industry standard.)*

> *Which capabilities have become less relevant and need to be "retired", and which ones are becoming increasingly critical?*

> *Are there any value-adding capabilities we currently lack that could become our undoing unless we develop or access them quickly?*

> *Do our specialised industry standard capabilities meet customer expectations of what an organization like ours should offer?*

> *And are there any weak points in our generic capabilities? After all, generic capabilities are like a football player's shoes. They won't win the game, but without them he can't play the game.*

Once we have placed these various capabilities on the Matrix we can rate them according to whether they are strong, adequate, weak or missing. We then use that rating to focus our investment on ensuring our capabilities are up to generating sustainable value. When using the Matrix, we always remember that a poor or missing capability powerfully reinforces the truth of the First Principle: *to generate sustainable value, your capabilities must continually align with conditions and opportunity-risk.*

After all, "continual alignment with conditions" is another way of saying "timing is everything." Investing in the right capability in a timely fashion means staying tuned to immediate and emergent conditions. When Blockbuster added more stores (capability) to an exponentially declining physical video market (conditions) they only lubricated their ride down the slippery slide of M.A.D. They figured more stores would add more value, but that was a dire miscalculation. It was simply the wrong investment at the wrong time.

The courage to retire a capability counts for a lot. Cash cows sometimes need to be put out to pasture. Unfortunately, it's rarely easy to retire a legacy capability. After all, it may have been the very foundation upon which an organization was built. And if we "go lean" we can still squeeze a few more drops out of the lemon. Seems reasonable, right? Not if the capability you refused to retire is left on your balance sheet and becomes a value-destroying stranded asset with no place left to go. No buyer, no value, no future. Just dead weight.

Consider the fossil fuels industry. Sure, while Tesla builds electric cars there may be a brief heightened demand for fossil fuel driven electricity. However, alternative energies like solar, thermal and wind are in an upward exponential growth swing. Plus, thanks to Tesla's new domestic range of low-cost battery technology, the generation and storage of electricity will soon become almost free.

Did we hear you whisper, *"Stranded assets?"*

We think so.

CONTROLLING THE BASKET

When you map out your core system of capability, it becomes so much easier to answer the only question that really matters: where should you focus your investment in order to generate sustainable value?

" *BETWEEN CALCULATED RISK AND RECKLESS DECISION-MAKING LIES THE DIVIDING LINE BETWEEN PROFIT AND LOSS.*"

Charles Duhigg

Tesla chose to go all in when it came to electric vehicles. It didn't bother with hybrid technologies or hydrogen cells. It was utterly *focused*. It picked a set of capabilities that added value over industry standard from the outset. And then it invested incredible amounts of human and financial capital into developing those capabilities.

Elon Musk once explained Tesla's culture of focus and calculated risk-taking like this: "It's ok to have your eggs in one basket as long as you control what happens to that basket."

MAKE THE WRONG INVESTMENT IN THE WRONG CAPABILITY, AND YOU RISK SELF-IMPOSED DISCONTINUITY. MAKE THE RIGHT INVESTMENT, AND YOU MIGHT BE STANDING ON THE CUSP OF SOMETHING REVOLUTIONARY.

Disruption Readiness Checklist #4

☐ We understand that capability is the engine of sustainable value-generation, and is therefore whatever an organization invests time or resources into developing or accessing.

☐ We understand that having cash and assets is not the same as having the right capabilities at the right time. We also know that assets that won't translate into capabilities fit for the future will almost certainly become stranded assets and destroy value.

☐ We understand that there are general, specialized, and value-adding capabilities, but the specialized and value-adding capabilities that come together in a system of core capabilities matter the most because they constitute our competitive advantage.

☐ We use tools like the Capability Matrix to measure and map out our core capabilities to ensure we are investing in the right capability at the right time.

| Power Up

CATALYTIC ACTIONS FOR EXPONENTIAL GROWTH

HOW A CATALYTIC ACTION CAN PRODUCE SYNERGISTIC OUTCOMES WITHIN DISRUPTIVE CONDITIONS, AND HOW UBER EXPERIENCED EXPONENTIAL GROWTH BY LAUNCHING EFFICIENT AND TIMELY CATALYTIC ACTIONS.

*" IN A LOT OF WAYS, IT'S NOT
THE MONEY THAT ALLOWS
YOU TO DO NEW THINGS.
IT'S THE GROWTH AND THE
ABILITY TO FIND THINGS THAT
PEOPLE WANT AND TO USE
YOUR CREATIVITY TO TARGET
THOSE."*

Travis Kalanick

THE ACCELERANTS

On March 13, 2012, the lights went out in Boston's Back Bay.

A three-alarm fire had broken out in a 115,000-volt transformer in a substation near the Back Bay Hilton, and the fire department was forced to cut the power. Authorities diverted underground trains and closed city streets as thick black smoke billowed over the area. Life in the well-heeled neighbourhood had come to a momentary standstill.

A few days later, a Tumblr called UberBoston published this post:

> *Whew, what a crazy 36 hours it's been. Two days of no power is no fun and living a couple blocks from the Hilton Back Bay myself, I can empathize. Along with 20k+ residents that have been without power, local bars, restaurants, and businesses have been feeling the effects of the outage.*
>
> *Now that things are back in action we want to make sure you're getting around Back Bay as conveniently*

and comfortably as possible. To help Back Bay #powerup, we're dropping our rates by 50% on any trip to/from the Back Bay tonight from 4pm until 4am tomorrow morning. If you're worrying about riding the T or finding a cab in Back Bay... DON'T! We'll get you wherever you need to go safely and in style. [...]

Let's pump some love back into the businesses affected by the outage and remind the Back Bay how much it means to us. Please help everyone out by tweeting your support to your favorite Back Bay businesses with the hashtag #PowerUp!

So what do you get when you add an upscale neighborhood, a three-alarm fire, a social media trend, and a transportation-disrupting start-up? An accelerant. At least, that's what Travis Kalanick would call it.

Four years earlier, fellow web entrepreneurs Kalanick and Garrett Camp were shooting the breeze on a winter night in Paris. Camp had recently sold his web discovery company StumbleUpon to Ebay and he was ready for another big challenge. In fact, he had a specific one in mind: he wanted to solve the horrendous cab service problem in San Francisco with an app that would allow users to simply push a button in order to get a car. Kalanick, who had recently sold his content-delivery company Red Swoosh, was battle-scarred from a decade of entrepreneurial vicissitudes. He didn't jump at the idea. He told Camp he didn't want to run a "limo company."

Camp forged ahead regardless. In 2009, he purchased the UberCab.com domain, and by the following summer, UberCab had a fully functioning app. However, in between creating the website and the app, he took back the reins of StumbleUpon from eBay. Too stressed out and pressed for time to properly lead the UberCab launch, he asked Kalanick to step in as "chief incubator" of the company.

Good thing for Camp and impatient riders all over the world that Kalanick had recovered his enthusiasm for the hustle by then. He took the job. His incubation tactics ushered Uber, the pugnacious poster child of the peer-to-peer revolution, into the world at an exponential clip. In five years, it grew from a domain and an app to an industry-disrupting juggernaut that may be worth as much as $50 billion USD today.

In 2010, the Uber solution—cars that come at the touch of a button—was a no-brainer. The timing seemed right: drivers in post-recession conditions were interested in earning extra money within the Uber network, and tech-savvy urban dwellers wanted their every experience to be app-enhanced. Plus, taxi service in cities like New York and San Francisco was notoriously frustrating, involving long waits, disgruntled cabbies, and haggles over credit cards and cash. Uber solved lots of problems for lots of people. The iron was decidedly hot, but how did Kalanick and his team strike?

The #PowerUp campaign in Back Bay was only one of many quick short jabs to the transportation status quo in cities across the US during Uber's launch into the disruption stratosphere. Like Apple with its "extraordinarily relevant" market segments, and Tesla with its "environmentalists and tech enthusiasts", Uber knew exactly who would launch their revolution. Rather than invest in expensive marketing campaigns, Uber decided to leverage the white-hot power of making well-to-do and highly networked people happy at critical moments.

By injecting their service into Twitter-trending episodes like the blackout in Back Bay, New Year's Eve in San Francisco, and sports events in Chicago, Uber drove potent word-of-mouth campaigns among influential early adopters. Tech-savvy and upwardly mobile users felt like high rollers when their sleek, black transport rolled up to the curb at the touch of a button. These trendsetters were happy to advertise their experience on social media, rapidly establishing Uber as an aspirational and very 21st century brand.

Kalanick's "accelerants"—real world situations in which early adopters faced acute versions of the problems Uber interventions were designed to solve— packed the launch with plenty of rocket fuel. Ultimately, the accelerant tactic became one of Uber's main word-of-mouth drivers, and in the Uber camp, word of mouth is sacred. That's because for every seven Uber rides, positive word of mouth creates another user.

#POWERUP, INDEED.

LIGHTWEIGHT CHAMPIONS

If a capability is defined as the right stuff to do a job, a catalytic action is defined as the best means of *getting it done*. It also calls for the least amount of resources, applied in a way that *punches above its weight*.

" *AN ORGANIZATION'S ABILITY TO LEARN, AND TRANSLATE THAT LEARNING INTO ACTION RAPIDLY, IS THE ULTIMATE COMPETITIVE ADVANTAGE."*

Jack Welch

In Chapter 6 we used the example of the B-movie star built for heavyweight class capability. While that image may characterize the strength of a capability required to generate value, the fighting style required for catalyzing action is more agile, and much more powerful.

Think martial arts. Think Bruce Lee.

Think about Lee's body and how he used it. His was a raw power expressed through a nearly scientific sense of grace. His frame was compact and his every movement was measured. He didn't waste any kinetic potential on swagger.

In other words, this quintessential lightweight's use of energy, force, and power was *catalytic*.

The impact of Lee's strike remained long after he executed it. He mustered energy that applied itself with more force than it had upon release. His energy became something *more* than what it was when he contained it in his body. In this way, he toppled foes twice his size.

In many ways, our beefcake B-movie hero is the perfect mascot for the industry heavyweights of the 20th century. He looks good, flexes often, and doesn't suffer from too much self-doubt. Plus, everything works out well for him because a team of scriptwriters gave him a very linear purpose. All he has to do is intercept the storm at the penultimate moment, and then he gets the girl.

But what if a couple hundred ninjas started descending from the ceiling? All of a sudden, the action is coming at Mr. Beefcake from every direction. It is more complex and chaotic. It's changing fast. How will his massive size help him in this scenario?

Picture today's disruptors as Lee-like lightweights who punch above their weight. Start-up champions like Uber use catalytic actions to topple lumbering, outsized competitors. The impact of their movements is synergistic, becoming something bigger once they are put into motion. Iterative, short bursts of focused action creating a domino effect that gradually—and then decisively—wears down their enemy to secure victory.

By contrast, bloated legacy organizations often bog down in complicating actions on protracted timelines. And frequently, their project management tools consume more management time than their actual projects. They stumble around, outsized and slow, easy prey for the next disruptive ninja to descend from their ceiling.

PAUSE AND CONSIDER: *How many of your organization's action plans seem incredibly complicated, and require too much time to fulfill?*

DEFINING CATALYTIC ACTION

A catalytic action is a targeted action that stimulates a system of capabilities. A well-designed catalytic action stimulates a system of capabilities and generates value. An *ideal* catalytic action stimulates and synergizes a system of capabilities that results in maximum value generation at minimum cost.

All catalytic actions produce real-world results (positive or negative) that allow you to gauge their fitness within conditions. Even a catalytic action that fails to deliver the expected outcomes is useful for the feedback it provides when it tests conditions. You may have assumed the conditions were "X" and the outcome was likely to be "A", but when you released the catalytic action the outcome was "C" which meant that the conditions were not what you assumed. This feedback is useful because pinging conditions with subtle interventions assists you with "reading the play" and seeing both the

> **" DO YOU WANT TO KNOW WHO YOU ARE? DON'T ASK. ACT! ACTION WILL DELINEATE AND DEFINE YOU."**
>
> *Thomas Jefferson*

correct and incorrect paths unfold. From there you make your next move.

PAUSE AND CONSIDER: *If we asked you to define a catalytic action at this stage, could you do it? How do you differentiate a catalytic action from a capability?*

For clarity's sake, let's take a trip through one revolution of the SiA algorithm, from beginning to end (keeping in mind that the SiA wheel never actually stops turning and there is therefore no real "beginning" or "end").

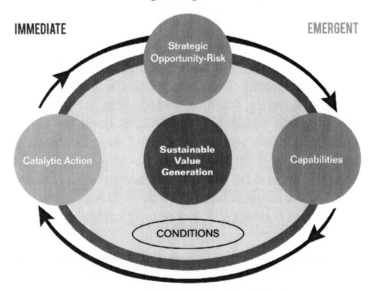

Diagram 7.1	**THE SIA ALGORITHM: A PERPETUAL MOTION**
	The SiA Algorithm is kept in perpetual motion by the continual updating of all five precepts to maintain strategy - in action.

Say it's late afternoon and you skipped breakfast (conditions). The immediate conditions tell you that you are hungry, and the emergent conditions tell you that you are due for football training at 6 pm. The idea of working another couple of hours while feeling hungry and then training on an empty stomach is a risk (pattern). This risk drives you to look for the opportunity to a) satisfy your hunger, and b) prime your body for football training.

You choose to make a protein shake and a healthy sandwich, and then take a 30-minute break (SOR). And clearly, you chose that SOR because you were asking, "What value do I want to generate?" And the answer was: "Satisfy my hunger, and be at my best for football training (value)."

So, off to the kitchen you go.

You open the refrigerator and take out the milk, cheese, salad, bread, butter, and ham (specialised capabilities for making a sandwich). Then you go to the kitchen drawer and select a paring knife, a butter knife, a plate, and a spoon (hygiene or generic capabilities used for all food preparation). While you are preparing your sandwich, you remember, "Oh yeah! The protein powder I just bought is state of the art and I'm the first one on my football team to have it." And there you have it: a potential leg-up over your teammates at training (a value-adding capability).

With all of your capabilities at hand, you take efficient catalytic actions to assemble your sandwich and super shake. Lunchtime prep, ninja-style.

But wait! You notice that the cheese is past its use-by date (condition). So you drop the cheese capability and go it alone with the ham. Thank heaven for the ability to ping conditions before committing so much energy to a sandwich that would have had the opposite effect of your super protein energizer.

After that close call you continue catalyzing action even to the point of adding another spoonful of protein powder to your shake while eating your sandwich. (You read on the label that for max effect, three spoonfuls is best.) This lunchtime SiA allows you to go through the process with little to no sunk costs. And there's no need to re-invest or start over if you need to make adjustments along the way.

Sandwich and shake in hand, you hit the sofa. Food gone, you grab a catnap. After thirty minutes, your hunger is gone and you're primed to start work again (immediate condition), and for training (emergent condition). You just used your innate SiA capability to be in an optimal state for the rest of your working day, and at your peak when you hit training.

Let's review:

1. **CONDITIONS:** Skipped breakfast, hungry, work to do, training later on
2. **PATTERN:** Working hungry, poor outputs, unfit for training, angry coach
3. **SOR:** Satisfy hunger and prepare for training by eating, drinking, and resting
4. **CAPABILITIES:** Cutlery and crockery (hygiene or generic), food items (specialized), and super protein powder (value-adding)
5. **CATALYTIC ACTION:** Iterative process of making sandwich and shake, checking and omitting the cheese, adding extra spoonful to shake, retiring to the sofa
6. **SUSTAINABLE VALUE GENERATED:** Satisfied hunger, rested, energy levels optimized for work and training, prepared to impress your coach and win a starting spot on the team

Once again, remember the First Principle: *to generate sustainable value, strategic opportunity-risk, capabilities and actions must continuously align with and within conditions.*

ANATOMY OF AN IDEAL CATALYTIC ACTION

Is there a way to break down what makes an ideal catalytic action tick? What does an ideal catalytic action *do*?

" I STILL BELIEVE IN SYNERGY, BUT I CALL IT NATURAL LAW."

Barry Diller

An ideal catalytic action produces the optimal intended outcome defined by your SiA. In the context of our lunchtime SiA, the catalytic action that allowed you to make lunch, rest, and prepare for training was the ideal catalytic action. En route to securing your optimal intended outcome, an ideal catalytic action stimulates a synergistic cascade of outcomes. That is, these outcomes produce a combined effect greater than the sum of their separate effects. They act like 1 + 1 equaling 3, not 2. Adding the extra spoonful of protein shake, which supplied additional protein to your brain, raised your blood sugar levels *and* eliminated food preparation time, was the catalytic action that gave you maximum bang for buck. It created multiple positive outcomes at once, and these outcomes worked together synergistically to make your workday and training prep as efficient and effective as possible.

In sum, an ideal catalytic action stimulates a system of events that result in maximum value generation at minimum cost. To do this—to create more with less, to fire up capabilities that act like 1 plus 1 equaling 3 (or much, much more)—catalytic actions must be *expedient*, *momentum building*, and *timely*. Let's take a closer look at each of these qualities.

Expedient

Let's revisit that hermetically sealed executive office where a five-to-ten year plan is being painfully gestated. In this slow-motion reality, elaborate documents are being created with columns dictating how they will manage and measure each step of the coming decade.

> "IN ENGLAND WE HAVE COME TO RELY UPON A COMFORTABLE TIME-LAG OF FIFTY YEARS OR A CENTURY INTERVENING BETWEEN THE PERCEPTION THAT SOMETHING OUGHT TO BE DONE AND A SERIOUS ATTEMPT TO DO IT."
>
> H.G. Wells

This approach is confined to linear timeframes, and doesn't allow for expedient, dynamic bursts of exponential action as conditions change.

The trajectory of a traditional plan is assumed to be predictable. There is a firm set of pre-conceived projects and actions. These plans are put into motion with careful and controlled behavior and an expectation that everything will elegantly cruise from one step to the next with guaranteed outcomes along the way. And if there are changes in the conditions along the way, they will be ignored because they might interfere with the "plan". Ultimately, this approach becomes more about working through whatever the plan dictates rather than achieving the desired end result in the most expedient manner available.

This is *plan-manage-measure*. And it's not the way the world works. Not anymore.

By contrast, catalytic actions are designed to be expedient, so that they move in the flow of exponentially accelerating time. That is, the lag time between formulating strategy and taking specific catalytic action is minimal, since we know conditions always shift. In a fast changing world, planning actions for the future based on an expectation that conditions will remain stable and predictable is a recipe for certain discontinuity.

PAUSE AND CONSIDER: *When you think about the actions your organization is currently discussing, which among them have the shortest time lag between planning and action?*

Remember that the SiA algorithm is a wheel that turns rapidly—rapidly enough to keep pace with the exponentially accelerating change cycles of the disruptive era. Turnover of decision-to-action has to be timely. Catalytic actions drive capability through SORs and conditions that are shifting with increasing velocity.

Momentum Building

Back to Mr. Lee, our quintessential lightweight champion. How did he topple foes twice his size? He created *momentum*.

> " *ABSORB WHAT IS USEFUL, DISCARD WHAT IS NOT, ADD WHAT IS UNIQUELY YOUR OWN.*"
>
> Bruce Lee

His moves were iterative in that they expend energy and drive force in short-bursts. Each time he struck, he took one rapid-fire yet mindful moment to observe the results of his action before he decided his next move. Each combination tested the conditions of the opponent and provided the feedback that allowed Lee to check state and adapt his approach so that it became progressively more devastating. Gradually, the cumulative effect of all of these striking combinations grew in force until it reached a tipping point and the fight was over.

This is the punch of SiA, and it's what separates a catalytic action from an item on a five-to-ten-year plan. The catalytic actions you take within the real-time wheel of SiA are iterative, just like Lee's moves. You make no over-investment in expenditure of energy. Rather, you execute your catalytic actions in short bursts in order to ping your conditions. The feedback you receive then allows you to shift your entire approach if need be. And because your catalytic actions are *expedient*, they are tuned with immediate and emergent conditions (rather than tacked to five-to-ten-year plans), and it's therefore *possible* to gauge the impact they are having within conditions. *Immediately.* You can actually test a variety of catalytic actions to see which ones create momentum within your conditions. Then you build upon the ones that do, and abandon the ones that don't.

PAUSE AND CONSIDER: *Which conditions impacting your organization could you ping with a low-investment catalytic action?*

Since by now Lee has beaten his sparring partner decisively, let's switch our focus and get back to nature. Remember Holling's forest from Chapter 1? This ecosystem is always moving in two directions: a forward loop of growth and conservation, and a backward loop of destruction and reinvention.

This "stable" zone where we go to feel a sense of time slowing down is actually a dynamic, continually evolving system. When you look at a centuries-old tree, it appears to be a totem of stability. And within a certain time frame, it is. But if you had eyes to see the full span of time in which this forest evolved, you would understand just how dynamic and iterative the life of this tree has been—and will always be.

Think of this tree in Hollings' forest as a seed that became a sprout that gained *momentum* until it was part of a whole system of trees. Centuries ago there were many other sprouts competing for development in the same soil. That soil was an arena of shifting conditions, including the weather patterns, other life forms in the region, and the sprouts themselves. As certain sprouts gained momentum within those conditions and became stems, other seeds and sprouts failed to take root and released their energy back into the soil, creating the organic matter that nurtured the stems. This cycle repeated itself as certain stems withered, enriching the *conditions* of the soil and fueling the momentum of the stems that eventually became an entire system of trees.

Grow and conserve. Release and reorganize.

Think of a successful business with a developed model, well-managed workforce, and powerful brand identity as an entity much like Hollings' forest. It may look like it emerged fully formed from the mind of some godlike visionary, but that's just not how it works. Like in the forest, iterative bursts of action created surges of momentum that tipped the system towards favoring a certain ecological makeup over others.

But iterative momentum building also works in reverse. Don't forget that spark of creative destruction. If this business possesses the wisdom of nature, it uses catalytic action from time to time to retire capabilities that are no longer required. Every now and then, it drops a branch to allow growth in other parts of the tree. Organizations can also use catalytic actions to build competitive capability that is disruptive to others. It only takes a small catalytic action that burns slowly and iteratively, growing in stature to become an all-consuming forest fire. In business, very small catalysts can quickly grow to raging proportions, transforming entire ecosystems. Upstart start-ups like Uber and Airbnb are doing just that.

Beware of large systemic projects that outweigh your organization's ability to deliver in sync with conditions. What may be a short, sharp jab for Apple may be an immense fight for a lesser organization. Traditional industries like manufacturing and construction can easily get locked into behemoth processes and large systemic projects that threaten their agility. These organizations are at risk of being taken apart by emerging global peer-to-peer start-ups with small-batch and micro-manufacturing capabilities. Even now, Chinese construction companies can use new manufacturing and construction techniques to build high-rise apartments in weeks and entire cities in months.

PAUSE AND CONSIDER: *Does your organization tend to adopt large-scale systemic projects or small-scale iterative actions? Why?*

Intervening in a system—disrupting it for its own good—only takes a sprout or a spark. A few short and sharp moves will work better than a tremendous investment into high-risk systemic overhaul. You opt for those high stakes actions only in the event of recovering an organization from M.A.D.

Have you ever seen an episode of the horrendous reality television show *Hoarders*? Distraught people accumulate lifetimes of junk that they will not (or cannot) part with, creating perilously unhealthy homes. In the span of an episode, mental health and "de-cluttering" professionals attempt to rehabilitate these homes—along with their mentally ill owners. Does it usually work out well?

No. Don't be a hoarder of legacy capability, presiding over a death trap organization. And if you are a professional charged with rehabilitating a M.A.D. hoarder's house through high-stakes overhauls, think deeply about what you keep and what you let go of. The choices you make could mean the difference between preserving capability that will provide a workable foundation for the future and simply hoarding more junk to throw out when the house is condemned.

Timely

Over the years, serial entrepreneur and Idealab founder Bill Gross has helped incubate hundreds of technology start-ups. He has presided over a number of totem-trees (eg. CitySearch), as well as

> **"YOU DON'T HAVE TO SWING HARD TO HIT A HOME RUN. IF YOU GOT THE TIMING, IT'LL GO."**
>
> *Yogi Berra*

a legion of sprouts that withered in the soil. A self-professed ideas guy, he always figured that the business concept—that inspired idea or "eureka moment" that the typical entrepreneur lives for— was the factor that mattered the most in terms of securing a start-up's failure or success. One day, he decided to test his theory.

He took dozens of Idealab and non-Idealab companies and scored them in terms of five factors: the business concept, the business model, the quality of the team executing it, the level of funding secured, and the timing of the whole shebang (the moment in history when the start-up launches).

Ideas-guy Gross was amazed by the results. According to his analysis, "timing" had more power to determine a start-up's fate than any other factor. At 42%, it easily edged out "team" (at 32%) and "idea" (at 28%). It would seem that the readiness of the market to embrace an idea mattered quite a bit more than the (debatable) quality of the idea itself. In other words, even if a business concept thrills a handful of eggheads with its elegance and logic, it won't count for much if the marketplace isn't—for various reasons—ready, willing, or interested at the time of launch. If immediate and emergent conditions don't smile upon the idea like rays of sun upon a fortuitous sprout, it will not gain the momentum it needs to grow.

Like we said in Chapter 6, timing *is* everything.

Catalytic actions that gain momentum are exquisitely timed. They are in the flow of exponentially accelerating time. Catalytic actions leverage disruptions before they have a chance to knock them into kingdom come. A well-conceived catalytic action catches a wave at the critical moment and that wave sends it surging upward rather than sinking below.

To capitalize on timing, you can do two things: pay special attention to early signs in your conditions, and ping conditions often. Pinging conditions means testing them with small catalytic actions to test whether the timing is right—and to relieve yourself of any misconceptions you may have about the reality of the conditions. This may involve a trial run at selling-in a capability to deliver value. Feel it out, fail fast, and move on. Watch out for the wild cards and weak signals. And be aware that those who can better organize their timing around conditions will be the winners.

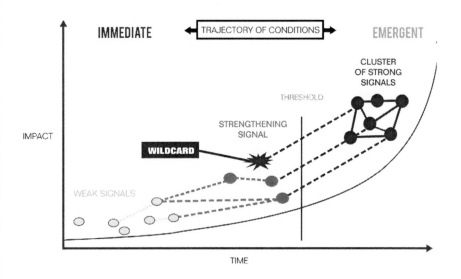

Diagram 7.2	**SIGNALS WITHIN EXPONENTIAL CHANGE**

Weak signals from emergent conditions strengthen to become strong signs of change as the exponential curve gathers pace. Initial conditions, many undefinable, gather in force to converge and pass through thresholds. Some through their own trajectory, some with the help of a wildcard that no one saw coming. From here there is no turning back. The conditions have clustered and the "long beginning to the shock awakening" has fully formed.

SiA—and the catalytic actions that emerge from the wheel of its algorithm—is fundamentally about working in a flow with exponentially accelerating change cycles. What happens when you're in the flow? You and your organization become your own accelerating change cycle, moving in sync with disruption, meeting exponential change with your own exponential actions. You hit your own exponential elbow. What does that look like?

Well, you will know a disruption-leveraging organization by the speed of its upward swing. Uber launched five years ago and today it's worth a reported $50 billion USD. In 2011 alone, Pinterest grew from 700,000 to 20 million users. In 2013, the RSS reader Feedly managed to triple its numbers from 4 million to 13 million in a single timely campaign to collect the users stranded by the dissolution of Google Reader.

PAUSE AND CONSIDER: *Which emerging conditions might indicate an opportunity for your organization to ride an exponential upswing?*

JUST DO IT

Fans of lore from the personal computing revolution love to tell the tale of Gary Kiddal, the inventor of the CP/M operating system and the man who could have been Bill Gates.

Kiddal, a revolutionary computer scientist who built his company Digital Research around the premise that microcomputers could be used for more than controlling equipment, didn't have a whole lot in common with Gates on a personal level. Where Microsoft Founder Gates was nebbish and withdrawn, Kiddal was a

" YOU NEVER KNOW WITH THESE THINGS WHEN YOU'RE TRYING SOMETHING NEW WHAT CAN HAPPEN. THIS IS ALL EXPERIMENTAL."

Richard Branson

freewheeling hippie with a taste for high-adrenaline sports. Gates was famous for being easy to admire but a little hard to like, and Kiddal was the cool guy, a kind of prototypical Richard Branson. But both men believed everyday people could operate computers at home, and both were poised to launch their brands into iconic territory based on this belief.

We may never know the true story of how Kiddal missed the opportunity to supply IBM with the operating system for the first PC. Some variations of the story paint Kiddal as a noble victim of the opportunistic Gates, and some depict him in less flattering terms. The legendary version usually takes the less flattering route.

That version goes like this: IBM pays Kiddal a visit in 1980, looking to strike a deal regarding use of his CP/M operating system in their first PC. Kiddal's wife receives the IBM folks while Kiddal is off flying his airplane. She dithers with the IBM folks about signing a non-disclosure agreement. By the time the lordly Kiddal touches down to meet the IBM folks, the deal has already gone south. Gates ends up buying Kiddal's OS. IBM completes the deal through Gates and the rest is disruption history.

Now, that may not be exactly how the great OS plot twist of 1980 went down, but it's a legend for a reason. Missed opportunities litter the highways and byways of disruption. Dithering is definitely not your best bet in a time of exponential surges. If timing is everything, missing a beat can be disastrous.

PAUSE AND CONSIDER: *When was the last time you dragged your feet on taking action and you ended up regretting it?*

Often, taking catalytic action is about *just doing it*. It's not science. It's not perfection. It's not about futzing around or deliberating an idea to death. It's taking a timely shot at a goal. Richard Branson probably says it best: "Screw it. Let's do it."

After all of this talk about acceleration, analysis, and alignment, we wouldn't be surprised if you had the impression you needed to be scientifically strategic to succeed. But that's not so. So before we forge ahead into discussing how you might complete one revolution of the SiA wheel by planning or logging some catalytic actions, let's get a few things straight.

First, taking catalytic action is like playing jazz. The weird notes keep it interesting. It's not like performing a symphony. Because catalytic actions are expeditious, momentum building, and timely, they allow you to work experimentally. Take a few short, sharp jabs. Try things to see where you gain traction. And if you have consistently kept abreast of conditions, your team has a shared understanding of those conditions, and you have identified SORs, value and capability, then *you are ready* to make agile and quick decisions. Experiment often in order to see how quickly the SiA wheel starts turning, and where it can take you.

Is a more conservative and measured approach sometimes more appropriate? Certainly. If your conditions are relatively static and the capability you want to execute is relatively simple, then a plan-manage-measure approach might be optimal. But in complex environments with shifting conditions, plan-manage-measure will more than likely create more problems than it solves. In those environments, you have to rely on your SiA capability, trust the work you have put in to align on conditions, SORs, value generation and capability, and *just do it*.

Lastly, the thing about SiA-style experimentation is that it runs on its own timeline. SiA observes Conditions Time rather than Calendar Time. Conditions don't care when your quarterly reports are due. They giveth SORs and taketh them away whenever they please.

A disruption-leveraging company like Netflix doesn't emerge according to a pre-determined timeline. They just ride on the back of the conditions that barrel down on the marketplace according to their own internal clock. Profit and loss doesn't necessarily occur within the arbitrary unit that is the financial year. A solid P & L may take 32.7 months to emerge as conditions allow.

Beware the quarterly results that are measured against a four-quarter annual plan as part of a five-year plan. It is arrogant and ignorant to suggest that value generation works in perfect sync with a calendar based on the seasons. The calendar might be a handy tool for selling bikinis and all-inclusive vacations, but it has limited value for organizations that are facing disruption in exponentially changing conditions.

PLANNING OR LOGGING CATALYTIC ACTIONS

" *THE PAINTING DEVELOPS BEFORE MY EYES, UNFOLDING ITS SURPRISES AS IT PROGRESSES. IT IS THIS WHICH GIVES ME THE SENSE OF COMPLETE LIBERTY, AND FOR THIS REASON I AM INCAPABLE OF FORMING A PLAN OR MAKING A SKETCH BEFOREHAND."*

Yves Tanguy

At this point, does it seem like we are advocating chaos? Good question.

Don't forget that in a time of disruption, the ability to tolerate and leverage chaos is a competitive advantage. Having said that, it is obviously best to change ahead of change in order to function in a relatively continuous manner. If your foresight and capability allows for change ahead of disruptive change, that is the preferred option.

Just like the SOR scoring parameters in Chapter 3, our catalytic action plan or log is a structure for nurturing and focusing SiA. It's not complicated—because it really can't afford to be.

First, you need to figure out what kind of conditions you're dealing with. For tame or stable conditions that are familiar and static, use the semi-traditional approach. Create an action plan, manage those items, and measure the results of each. And if you've read the conditions right, all will be well. After all, in a well-known neighborhood you don't complicate crossing the road.

But if you assess conditions and they appear to be in a state of flux, adapt your approach accordingly. In dynamic conditions, don't map out actions according to a set timeline. Your plan may have an initial starting action (a first "punch") with a desired outcome and completion date in mind. But the middle should be experimentation-friendly. This will feel more like trekking through an unknown winter forest than crossing a familiar road.

Between initiation and completion, identify the next iterative action in the wake of the last. As you do this, generate a log of the actions you took and the outcomes they produced. Where a set action plan tells a project in advance exactly what it needs to look like, a log tells the story of the project as it actually unfolded. It helps you to keep an eye on the endgame rather than be held captive by it. It also allows you to be opportunistic and take advantage of the conditions as they unfold, and to mitigate or manage previously unknown risks as they emerge. In most cases, the outcome will either be the early demise of the catalytic action plan, or a catalytic action plan that succeeded beyond all expectations.

We like to tell the story of the two newbie climber colleagues who were excited at the prospect of photographing an eclipse from atop a high mountain. One got up early to hustle down to the climbing gear store to get all the equipment he needed for the climb. The other took it easy. After a hearty breakfast, she made her way down to the store.

By the time she arrived, her colleague had already been gone for two hours, gear in hand. He had a climb plan that would see him at the peak of the mountain in four hours, ready to capture the shot. He figured there was no way his colleague was going to arrive on time, so he would grab the scoop. She would have to buy the shots from him.

She arrived at the store, had a look around, and couldn't resist chatting to the well-climbed sales assistant. He told her all about the mountain: the best faces to climb, the dangers to avoid, and the rest spots along the way. She listened, smiling politely, and then said, "Let's cut to the chase. What's the fastest way to the top of the mountain?" The assistant, a little taken aback, replied, "Actually, we offer a helicopter service. I can have you up there in twenty minutes." And just like that, she had her ascension plan.

Thirty minutes later she was cheerfully photographing the eclipse. Her colleague had taken a wrong turn and arrived late. In fact, by the time he scrambled to the top, he was not only worn out but he had missed the shot entirely. And the best part was that she had first learned about the helicopter months ago when she conducted a Conditions Analysis. She only quizzed the sales assistant to figure out if there was an even better way of getting to the top.

Who do you think ended up selling the shot to whom?

ANYTHING IN FIVE MINUTES

When the *Wall Street Journal* asked Kalanick how he dealt with the exponential growth of his company, he said: "I have a list of the hardest, most challenging problems that our company needs to solve and I start at the top and work my way down. And I have a list of the coolest most fascinating things that we can invent and I start at the top of the list and I work my way down."

> " *ALL LIFE IS AN EXPERIMENT. THE MORE EXPERIMENTS YOU MAKE THE BETTER.* "
>
> *Ralph Waldo Emerson*

What does that list look like? What story would Kalanick's catalytic action log tell?

Uber is one of many companies meeting exponential change with exponential action. From Kalanick's description, it seems like there is plenty of fun and fascination to be had on the trip to the top. Tactics like paring down marketing costs, striking decisively at opportunities for accelerated growth, and solving problems for the right communities at the right times have opened the elevator doors of the exponential era for Uber. And nobody can say what the top floor looks like.

As Kalanick puts it, "If we can get you a car in five minutes, we can get you anything in five minutes." He and his team are still pinging the delivery and transportation industries by launching products like food-delivery services and ride-sharing solutions that carry on the Uber tradition of puckish disruption. It makes us wonder how many other "cool, fascinating" items are on Kalanick's list?

Disruption Readiness Checklist #5

☐ We understand that the purpose of a catalytic action is to stimulate a synergistic system of events that help us to build or access capability at minimum cost.

☐ We understand that the ideal catalytic action is expedient, momentum building, and timely.

☐ We use iterative bursts of low-investment catalytic actions to ping conditions, test our beliefs, and determine the most efficient route to generating value.

☐ We plan-manage-measure when conditions are tame, but when conditions are dynamic, we simply log our actions to keep a record of which ones worked best for helping us drive capability to generate value.

CHAPTER 8	SiA Revolution
	STRATEGY, HUMANITY AND COMMUNITY

WHAT IT MEANS TO BE RATHER THAN DO STRATEGY, HOW THE HUMAN CONDITION UNDERPINS AND VALIDATES ALL STRATEGIC ENDEAVORS, AND HOW THE POINT OF ALL OF THIS IS LIFE.

" *IT WAS FILMLESS PHOTOGRAPHY,
SO MANAGEMENT'S REACTION
WAS, 'THAT'S CUTE, BUT DON'T
TELL ANYBODY ABOUT IT.'"*

Steve Sasson

STEVE'S KODAK MOMENT

Kodak's problem was never a lack of good ideas. In fact, when it filed for Chapter 11 bankruptcy in 2012, the iconic technology company owned an estimated $2 Billion in intellectual property. At this bitter juncture, good ideas were literally Kodak's primary asset, the best remnant of value the company had to show for its decades of market dominance. And naturally, these good ideas hadn't been dredged up from a mine, harvested from a field, or assembled in a plant. They came from Kodak's people.

People like Steve.

In December 1975, electrical engineer Steve Sasson and his lab assistant Jim Schueckler had been tinkering with an experimental chip called the charge-coupled device for about a year. His bosses at Kodak had given him the chip more or less to keep him busy. It seemed to be an effective strategy.

Sasson was completely taken with the "CCD", which held out the promise of converting light into electrical charges that could be stored as data. He figured he could use it to create a handheld camera that was capable of taking "filmless photographs." The project was especially appealing to Sasson because he knew such a camera would require little to no moving mechanical parts. He was a fervent inventor but that didn't mean he had much in the way of a mechanic's prowess.

Using spare parts from a used part bin in a Kodak research lab, Sasson and Schueckler eventually built a toaster-sized 3.6-kilogram camera that still counted as hand-held if you didn't mind engaging in a little upper body conditioning while you snapped pictures. The cumbersome marvel used the CCD to record images onto a digital tape that Sasson could pop in and out. During the design phase, Sasson had decided to make the tape capable of holding 30 images. He figured the ability to store more would make his invention even more difficult to understand than it already was.

With all of the elements in place, Sasson and Scheukler were ready to test their prototype. They looked at each other and decided to find a more inspiring subject.

Fortunately, Joy Marshall was working.

Sasson and Scheukler found the comely lab tech seated at a Teletype, her dark hair forming a striking silhouette against a white background. She was seemingly all ready for her close-up. Marshall agreed to let the two furtive characters from the back of the lab take her picture with their monstrous contraption. Sasson snapped a headshot that took 23 seconds to record.

Back in their corner of the lab, they displayed the resulting image on the screen of a playback unit. The silhouette was there—miraculous black on white—but the details of Marshall's face had somehow not completed the journey. Still, the two inventors were ecstatic, all congratulations and high fives. They knew there were countless reasons why there should be no image at all. They built the first digital camera and it actually worked.

Marshall's review was a little less glowing: "Needs work."

Pic 8.1 | **STEVE SASSON RECEIVES THE NATIONAL MEDAL OF TECHNOLOGY AND INNOVATION**

In November 2010 US President Barack Obama presented the National Medal of Technology and Innovation to Steven Sasson during a ceremony in the East Room of the White House in Washington, DC. Steve received the award for his invention of the digital camera.   Photo: REUTERS/Kevin Lamarque

She turned tail and left the inventors to revel alone. She missed the moment when Sasson switched a pair of wires around and her face suddenly came through in brilliant resolution on the playback screen. Hers was the face of history smiling at them indulgently, a black and white headshot of a revolution to come.

Before long, Sasson was demonstrating his prototype to Kodak brass. He was excited to explain how it worked and ready to answer a barrage of technical questions. But those questions never came. The conversation went a little differently than he'd imagined it would. Sasson was asked what he thought the ramifications of his filmless camera would be. He admitted that he had no idea.

But Kodak did.

THE WHEELS

How many times has a human spirit been ground underneath the wheels of misguided continuity? Once the multinationals of the 20th century gained a certain amount of mass and momentum, how easy was it for them to roll right over the type of thinking responsible for creating them? At what point did the *modus operandi* of corporate bureaucracy and legacy capability dwarf the competitive advantage of unrestrained creativity?

> " *THE SEED OF REVOLUTION IS REPRESSION."*
>
> Woodrow Wilson

As John F. Kennedy once said, "Those who make peaceful revolution impossible will make violent revolution inevitable."

Is this disruptive age serving up a kind of revolutionary comeuppance on behalf of creative human beings? In this time when small dismantles big, continuity gives way to discontinuity, and leveraging disruption generates value, M.A.D. organizations seem to be getting their just desserts. Because they couldn't choose peaceful revolution— leveraging disruption, changing ahead of change, releasing and reorganizing—they are getting a taste of something much more violent.

Kodak saw Steve Sasson as a staff member. But that's not who he was. Sasson was his own accelerating change cycle within an organization that failed to recognize the impact he could have on it. Sasson lit a disruptive spark and Kodak tried to stomp it out. But it simply escaped the confines of the organization to light the world around it on fire. By the time the digital wildfire reached Kodak, it was a world-destroying inferno, and they were just so much legacy tinder.

Cameras didn't matter. Film didn't matter. Assets didn't matter. Management didn't matter. Legacy didn't matter.

Only Steve mattered.

We are inviting you to recognize how much *you* matter. We are inviting you to think SiA, act SiA, and *be* SiA. Read immediate and emergent conditions, perceive strategic opportunity-risks, identify sustainable value, develop capabilities, and take catalytic actions. Then do it all over again. In fact, don't ever stop. Let the wheel of SiA keep revolving so that it can keep up with the accelerating change cycles of the disruptive era. Realize that the SiA wheel never stops turning—its revolution is constant, like the forward and backward loops of Hollings' deceptively "stable" forest. And if you choose to move in sync with the wheel of SiA—if you choose to honor your own status as a living change cycle capable of influencing history itself— then you will truly be generating SiA.

After a while, once you've started to really generate SiA, feel free to forget all about it. Seriously—at some point down the road forget all the terminology and the algorithmic steps we taught you. Instead, *internalize* SiA. *Be* SiA. Allow the concepts upon which we constructed our algorithm to change the way you think about the world and your place in it. And by the time you notice that this is happening, it really won't matter whether you use the same vocabulary we use. All that will matter is the benefit you derived from learning it.

What is that benefit?

YOU WILL NO LONGER BELIEVE YOU ARE A COG IN A MACHINE YOU CAN'T CONTROL. YOU WILL UNDERSTAND THAT YOU—LIKE STEVE JOBS, JOHN MACKEY, MARC TARPENNING, ELON MUSK, GARRET CAMP, TRAVIS KALANICK, STEVE SASSON, OR ANY OF THE DISRUPTIVE ERA'S INSTIGATORS—ARE YOUR OWN WHEEL. AND LIKE ANY WHEEL, YOU ARE BUILT FOR REVOLUTION.

GENERATING SIA

" *WE ARE THE MIRACLE OF FORCE AND MATTER MAKING ITSELF OVER INTO IMAGINATION AND WILL. INCREDIBLE. THE LIFE FORCE EXPERIMENTING WITH FORMS. YOU FOR ONE. ME FOR ANOTHER. THE UNIVERSE HAS SHOUTED ITSELF ALIVE. WE ARE ONE OF THE SHOUTS.*"

Ray Bradbury

Before we *completely* dispense with teaching or learning vocabulary, let's take a moment to consider the word "generation."

Value *generation*, at the center of it all. *Generating* SiA. In the words of the First Principle: *to generate sustainable value, opportunity-risk, capabilities and actions must continuously align with and within conditions.*

We chose to place the word "generate" at the heart of our algorithm for a specific reason. *Generate* is a 16th century word meaning "to beget offspring", from the Latin word *generatus*, which is the past participle of *generare*, "to beget, produce". "Generation" is *making life*. We are very actively aligning SiA with the life force itself. And why shouldn't we? Real life—and the astounding, joyful, challenging, and perilous experiences that constitute it—is what we are concerned with when we *generate* strategies.

Remember that when we talk about value generation, we are never simply referring to profit margins. We're talking about *creating*. We're talking about providing something indispensable to the value networks that surround you and support your very existence. We're talking about changing the world in order to make it a more hospitable, abundant, and joyful place for this network. Value supports *life*. Authentically generating value means living an infinitely more interesting and prosperous life.

Picture that hermetically sealed executive office one more time. That office by itself is an antithetical zone of *generating SiA*. It's situated at the opposite pole of the strategizing experience we are recommending for vital, creative people poised on the brink of exponentially accelerating opportunity-risk. It's anti-*life*.

Strategy isn't just something to *do*, a milestone on the slow trek to corporate numbness. Generating SiA is about gathering the vital energies of a team and focusing them to generate powerful outcomes. It's about the life force expressing itself joyfully as leaders and team members recover their sense of creative purpose. It's about giving people the power to change.

Strategist and SiA practitioner Paul Houghton puts it like this: "Sometimes you need a strategy that will give you lift off from the 'mundane now.'"

Houghton was once called in to help an Australian charity deal with that perennial problem of all non-profits everywhere: government shifts causing financial uncertainty. Were they a tight enough operation? How could they work harder to get that money? Where were the weak spots in their plan of attack?

Actually, what Houghton discovered was that the organization was a well-oiled machine when it came to securing funds. In fact, they had become a little too good at pushing the paper to win those tenders. That proficiency had, over time, transformed the charity's culture from a passionate, purpose-driven group into a mirror reflection of the government bureaucracies funding them. Paper-pushing was the pivot around which their "mundane now" endlessly turned.

In other words, they had become the sort of organization where the life force goes to die a slow death from a thousand paper cuts. And in the end, there wasn't much Houghton could do for them. M.A.D. had taken its toll and "strategy" remained a box that merely needed ticking.

But then there's Exhibit B: the Southern Metropolitan Cemeteries Trust, a not-for-profit charged with maintaining and preserving eight historic cemeteries in Victoria, Australia. This group took SiA and ran with it, achieving definite lift-off from their previous strategic approach.

In 2013, the SMCT was preparing to update their strategic plan. Jane Grover, who was then the deputy of CEO Jonathan Tribe, decided to attend an executive forum where I (Larry) happened to be speaking. Hearing about the significance of conditions analysis resonated with her, and she convinced Tribe to meet with Resilient Futures. Before long, SMCT was embarking on a yearlong journey to embed the SiA framework into the entire organization. It was a year that transformed the culture and thinking of the organization, laying the groundwork for sales increases and innovations that led the Australian cemeteries sector. The program designed for SMCT was titled "SMCT: Change Ahead of Change", and since its implementation, that is exactly what they have been doing.

"The way the group operated before we worked with SiA, it was that typical not-for-profit culture," says Tribe. He had already put his management team through accountability-oriented management training, but he seized upon the SiA model as an opportunity to give the team some much-needed technical capability. He wanted to "embed, right into the depths of the organization, something that would help them resolve their planning issues, so that, if for example they wanted to go out and buy a new piece of equipment, they would first run it through the SiA algorithm and think about it in terms of the big picture."

SMCT's big picture was this: if they were going to stay competitive in a rapidly changing regulatory and commercial milieu, they needed to release and re-organize.

For SMCT, "changing ahead of change" meant launching SORs that would position them to benefit from changes in the cultural, demographic, business, and political conditions. To begin with, the baby boomers representing their next big wave of clients had different notions about life and death than past generations. They wanted to celebrate rather than memorialize, and SMCT had to ensure its products and marketing reflected that new generational ethos.

Secondly, in other states, cemeteries were being deregulated, providing the opportunity (and risk) of expanding the roles cemetery-operators could assume in their service to the community. SMCT believed it was only a matter of time before deregulation would broaden *their* possibilities. They needed to ensure their capabilities would be up to the challenge when that time came. So they launched a series of SORs, mustering entrepreneurial capabilities that surprised and inspired them. In the end, the pay-off went way beyond profit margins.

Nowadays, says Grover (who is now the SMCT CEO), her organization is "no longer a passive brand." She claims embedding the SIA algorithm "transformed our understanding of flexibility, agility, and timing. We have confidence to pursue opportunities and mitigate risks. We have rigor in our processes. And we have a common strategic language and framework."

Embedding SiA was more than a strategic planning process for SMCT. The entire SMCT team was involved in formulating and embracing a strategic culture, with front-end ownership and genuine passion. They made it a permanent part of their organizational psyche, a new style of thinking and communicating. SiA was the wheel that began turning in their imaginations, transporting them to unexplored territories.

CHANGE AHEAD OF CHANGE WASN'T A SERIES OF BOXES FOR MANAGEMENT AND BOARD TO TICK OFF. IT WAS A CAMPAIGN TO SECURE THEIR FUTURE.

BE THE STRATEGY

Jane Monk, the director of an Australian government department, remembers the stiffness of her team's initial Resilient Futures-facilitated strategic planning sessions. They were operating in a climate of government austerity and staff cutbacks, so in general the mood around the office was tense, withdrawn. The communication didn't exactly flow.

> " *COMMUNICATION LEADS TO COMMUNITY, THAT IS, TO UNDERSTANDING, INTIMACY AND MUTUAL VALUING.*"
> Rollo May

"But something happened," says Monk. "We just got to know each other. There were all of these capabilities we had that we weren't aware of previously. We had so much more alignment around values—especially the value we felt we could offer to our stakeholders—than we realized."

The revelations of Jane's colleagues echo those of GM Holden's engineering talent in Chapter 6. They realized their communication problems didn't remain within the boundaries of their team; they manifested externally, hampering their capacity to do good work in their value network. They realized they needed to do a far better job communicating with internal and external stakeholders.

So how did they act on this revelation? One of the SORs they pursued was exploring the way new technologies could support their mission to communicate more clearly with the community. How could technology help them to become impassioned storytellers rather than harried bureaucrats ticking boxes on community engagement checklists? They discovered that 3-D modeling software helped them to create much more vivid and relevant presentations than the slide shows and spreadsheets of yesteryear.

"We used to deal with people in a much more linear fashion," says Monk. "But we're connecting with communities facing change. It's really important. So we need to help people see what they need to see. The 3-D modeling has allowed us to do that."

Jane's team epitomizes a trend we've seen play out again and again. The movement from "doing strategy" to "being strategy" runs on a singular and particularly potent fuel: people getting to know—and *enjoy*—each other. That takes time—and sometimes more time than people have the appetite for.

As US based SiA practitioner and innovation expert Kip Bergstrom says, "Americans can be like, 'Ready, aim, fire! What's the project?'" That attitude of fire-breathing impatience to get to the project, the pay-off, and the end game can cause a team to bypass critical collective growth. Team members who dislike or distrust one another rarely generate effective strategies. A team that is ignorant as to the capabilities that exist within their organization will be blind to their strategic possibilities.

But when a team collectively learns and activates SiA, they start to behave like a flock of birds. Their strategic formation is effortless, intuitive, and evolving as a real-time response to the changing environment. With SiA in full flight, the algorithm cascades throughout the organizational ecosystem so that all team-members use a common language and framework for strategizing, problem-solving, and performance evaluation. They are all attuned to SORs and they share what they perceive. They naturally "braille the future," as Bergstrom likes to say, "and flow with the game as it emerges for them."

Kip also likes to remind us of the words of one of the greatest ice-hockey players of all time, Wayne Gretzky: "A good hockey player plays where the puck is. A great hockey player plays where the puck is going to be." Playing where the game has already happened will get you nowhere, but getting ahead of where the game will be is an approach worth cultivating. "The Great One" did it all on his own, and elevated his team members in the process. But doing it effectively within SiA requires a team moving towards emerging conditions in formation.

Teams like Grover's, Monk's, and Bergstrom's know each other, talk to each other, and organically strategize together. Their healthy habits radiate outward, improving communication with other stakeholders in their value networks. The sense of trust and positive intention is infectious. The SORs that express the naturally occurring values within their organizations seem to present themselves unbidden. Authenticity flows.

THE SECOND PRINCIPLE

Now that our journey through SiA is at an end, we are finally ready to share its second (and last) principle: work *with* the human condition. To put it another way: if you don't understand humans and work with them through standing in their shoes, you'll never be a great strategist.

> " *IDEALISM IS LIKE A CASTLE IN THE AIR IF IT IS NOT BASED ON A SOLID FOUNDATION OF SOCIAL AND POLITICAL REALISM.*"
>
> *Claude McKay*

Think about the last time you heard a discussion about sustainability. We find denial over the reality of the human condition readily flows in this context. For example, we can recall a dubious climate change solution proposed by a participant at a Resilient Futures forum: "All we need to do is get people to stop driving cars."

Or how about corporate flights of fancy over "authentic" team values? Those are usually fertile breeding grounds for misguided notions flowing from executive-sanctioned spin. I remember a senior official once declaring, "Our people are committed to this organization," when the micro-conditions suggested nothing could be further from the truth.

It doesn't matter if it's the "right thing", the "smartest move", the "most logical way forward", or the "obvious action". If real human beings are not engaged, aligned, and committed to implementing the strategy, it's DOA. The human condition is the great defeater of all superior strategies. Culture *does* trump strategy. However, the strategist who works *with* the human condition is a supreme activator, marshalling authentic energies towards attainable outcomes.

Remember Peter Vawdrey, GM Holden's SiA expert? Sometime after his adventures in the automotive industry, he spent time in the Philippines, overseeing the product engineering development branch of a global aerospace company. There, in Baguio City, his strategist's capabilities came in handy.

When he started out with the company, they were suffering from an acute case of brain drain. The company attracted the best and brightest, since its computer-controlled manufacturing machines could only be operated by highly skilled workers with four to five years of training under their belts. But that rich skill base had become an Achilles' heel, making the organization a target for overseas companies looking to poach well-trained technicians.

The consequences were dire. In six months, they had lost 15% of their workforce. Operators with as little as three months' experience were using—and breaking—million-dollar machines that cost $50,0000 to repair. What SORs could turn the situation around?

Naturally, understanding the conditions was critical. "In the Philippines, if you leave the country to make it big overseas, you are considered a hero," explains Vawdrey. That cultural condition—the *human* condition—made it relatively easy for overseas companies to squire those technicians off to new lives in novel climes.

That insight made the right SOR simple, even ingenious. The company simply had to update their recruiting target. Instead of seeking young males, they needed to hire mature females. Women with families and deep roots in their country. Women who were decidedly less attracted to the concept of playing the expatriate hero. It was a calibration of the human element that worked like a charm.

Understanding the human condition—being able to assess what people think, feel, and need—is an indispensable capability in the generation of SiA. Without it, good luck.

Remember Abby Harris, our alternative fuels association CEO from Chapter 3? She ultimately became the leader of a different and considerably larger national association—but one with problems that were remarkably similar to the ones that dogged her last association. They had fights over process, confusion over strategy, and plenty of wheel-spinning. Prior to her arrival, board and management had participated in a one-day strategic planning workshop. The only real outcome Harris could identity was a piece of software the consultants had given the previous CEO. They told him to populate the software with every action he took. He smiled, nodded, and cut them a check.

The association's strategic plan sat on the shelf, collecting dust—along with a rather expensive piece of software.

Fortunately, by this time in her career, the SiA wheel revolved smoothly and continually in Harris' mind. She was able to lead the team through a process that led to breakthroughs, revelations, and a business plan with strategic priorities that seemed preternaturally obvious.

In a past life, Harris was an engineer. With SiA, it seemed as if she finally had a tool for strategy that complemented her logical sensibilities. She says, "It just gelled with me. It's not static. We check it at intervals to make changes. We keep testing whether it makes sense."

Well-intended tactics—from CEO-tracking software to feel-good "visioning" exercises—that are laughably out of step with human realities are not logical. Strategies that run on wishful thinking, spin, or unfounded expectations sit on the shelf, collecting dust. There's nothing quite so pathetic as a "value or mission statement" or a "brand platform" that bears no resemblance to the actual, authentic culture of a corporation or the impact it has on the world around it.

But work *with* the human condition and soon enough you will be working *for* the human condition. Teams that work in sincere alignment on campaigns to secure the future are living life to the fullest. They enjoy what they do and who they do it with. Like Kalanick, they have lists full of "cool, fascinating" projects. Like Harris, they are gratified by the fitness of their tools for the task at hand.

They have *fun*.

THE REVOLUTION NEVER STOPS

To generate sustainable value, opportunity-risk, capabilities, and actions must continuously align with and within conditions. Work with the human condition. These are the only two principles of SiA.

That's really all we need to remember.

In this era of disruption, when technology, connectivity, complexity, chaos, and change cycles are driving exponential change forward at an alarming pace, very little can be taken for granted. Your ability to leverage disruption is your best bet for riding high on the crest of these historic changes. It's also your opportunity to move forward in a spirit of purpose, creativity, and intimacy with your traveling companions.

> " *FROM A CERTAIN POINT ONWARD THERE IS NO LONGER ANY TURNING BACK. THAT IS THE POINT THAT MUST BE REACHED.* "
>
> *Franz Kafka*

SiA is a wheel that never stops turning, because it was built for a world that never stops changing. As the world is revolutionized around you, use SiA as a tool for your own revolutionary outcomes. Be a participant. Meet exponential change by changing exponentially. Read immediate and emergent conditions, perceive strategic opportunity-risks, generate sustainable value, develop capabilities, and take catalytic actions. Then do it again. And again. Don't stop. Life doesn't stop. Keep up with life.

Just like Hollings' forest which continually evolves in its backwards and forwards loops, your life is an expression of flux. You are a change cycle among change cycles. Even when many factors of disruption are accelerating at a dizzying pace, never forget that you are a product of this time in history. With determination, insight, and faith, it is possible for you to keep up with disruption—and even better—to generate *life* in the midst of it.

YOU WERE MADE FOR THIS.

GLOSSARY OF KEY TERMS AND DEFINITIONS

ADAPTIVE CYCLE: *The observation by Buzz Hollings of change moving in two directions: a forward loop of growth and conservation, and a backward loop of release and reorganization—helping us to understand when to reap rewards, and when to foster destruction and innovation.*

AGILITY: *The knowledge, insight, creativity, commitment, and decision-making that allows for timely releasing, re-thinking and reorganizing in sync with changing conditions.*

ALGORITHM: *A process or set of rules to be followed in calculations or other problem-solving operations.*

ALIGNMENT: *A state of agreement or cooperation with a common cause or viewpoint.*

AMBIGUITY EFFECT: *The tendency to avoid options for which missing information makes the outcome seem "unknown".*

ARBITRAGE: *Taking on risk you can cover but laying off a proportion of that risk to other parties.*

AUTHENTIC: *A state of being genuine and representative of the facts, rather than false or copied.*

AUTHENTICITY: *The degree to which on is true to one's own personality, spirit or character, despite external pressures.*

AVAILABILITY CASCADE: *A self-reinforcing process in which a collective belief gains more and more plausibility through its increasing repetition in public discourse (otherwise known as "repeat something long enough and it will become true").*

BANDWAGON EFFECT: *The tendency to do (or believe) things because many other people do (or believe) the same (also known as "groupthink").*

BOND: *Authentic connection, understanding and exchange of value in a trusted manner.*

BRAND: *Any feature that identifies one's product or service as distinct from another and links to memory, recall and perception.*

BUSINESS AS USUAL (BAU): *The normal execution of operations within an organization.*

BUSINESS MODEL: *The means by which an organization creates, delivers and captures value.*

CAPABILITY: *The ability to do something.*

CAPABILITY MATRIX: *An SiA tool to assist in the timely identification of, and investment in, the capability to maintain sustainable value generation.*

CAPACITY: *The amount or size of a capability.*

CATALYST: *Something introduced to a network or system that stimulates change and scales after the stimulus has been withdrawn.*

CATALYTIC ACTION: *A targeted action that stimulates a system of events that leverages synergistic outcomes (e.g. 1+1=53); thus achieving more with less to produce an optimal, intended outcome.*

CHAOS: *The rate of discontinuity in a system or network.*

COGNITIVE BIAS: *A pattern of deviation in judgment, whereby inferences about other people and situations may be drawn in an illogical fashion.*

CONFIRMATION BIAS: *The tendency to search for, interpret, focus on and remember information in a way that confirms one's preconceptions.*

COMMITMENT: *To take action to make something happen.*

COMPETENCY: *The level or standard of ability achieved in a capability.*

COMPLEXITY: *A term generally used to characterize something with many parts where those parts interact with each other in multiple ways.*

CONDITIONS: *The factors or prevailing situations influencing performance or outcomes.*

CONDITIONS ANALYSIS: *The systematic collection and interpretation of data and information that informs an organization's view of the factors that will (or may) influence their performance or outcomes.*

CONDITIONS MAP: *A Conditions Map is a visual and verbal representation of the various conditions that are defining an organization's immediate and emergent state of affairs. It identifies the primary conditions existing at the micro, macro, or mega scale.*

CONNECTIVITY: *The state of being connected or interconnected.*

CONTINUITY: *The unbroken and consistent existence or operation of something over time; a state of stability and the absence of disruption.*

CONTINUOUS CHANGE: *Change that is expected and uninterrupted, and tends to follow certain patterns (e.g. day and night, the seasons, aging).*

CORE CAPABILITIES: *Those capabilities critical to locking-in value and generating sustainable value.*

CHANGE CYCLE: *The time it takes for a process to be complete (eg. the time it takes to change something, to learn and apply something, to produce something, to complete a transaction).*

CHECK STATE*: To take a timeout to check the state or condition of a SiA.*

CRASH TEST DUMMY SYNDROME: *To continually be blind-sided and disrupted by discontinuous change before reorganizing and repeating the process.*

CREATIVE DESTRUCTION: *The process of industrial mutation that incessantly revolutionizes the economic structure from within (Joseph Schumpeter).*

CYCLE TIME: *The period taken to complete a cycle through the SiA algorithm.*

DISCONTINUITY: *The state of having intervals or gaps; lack of continuity.*

DISCONTINUOUS CHANGE: *Change that is disruptive, unforeseen and uncertain.*

DISINTERMEDIATE: *The reduction in the use of intermediaries between producers and consumers. For example by buying online from a manufacturer rather that from a retailer the retailer is disintermediated; "cutting out the middlemen".*

DISORIENTATION: *To lose direction or position.*

DISRUPTED: *To be interrupted (by an event, activity, or process); causing a disturbance or problem.*

DISRUPTION: *disturbances or problems that interrupt an event, activity, or process.*

ELBOW (OF EXPONENTIAL CHANGE): *The point in an exponential curve when the rate of change begins to accelerate.*

EMERGENT: *In the process of coming into being or becoming prominent; arising as an effect of complex causes and not understood through analysis as the sum of the combined effects.*

ENGAGEMENT: *To be interested in something.*

ENTREPRENEUR'S DELIGHT: *See – Arbitrage.*

EXPONENTIAL CHANGE: *An increase or compounding change becoming more and more rapid.*

FIELD OF ALL KNOWLEDGE: *A concept designed to illustrate all of the knowledge available to us, in a simple diagram. It describes three domains of knowledge. What we know we know, what we know we don't know, and what we don't know we don't know; and at times, what we don't want to know we know.*

FIRST PRINCIPLE: *the fundamental concepts or assumptions on which a theory, system, or method is based.*

FIXED ACTION PATTERN (FAP): *A learned or instinctive behavioral sequence that is often hard wired into some species.*

FIRST PRINCIPLE OF SIA: *To generate sustainable value, strategic opportunity-risk, capabilities and actions must continuously align with and within conditions.*

GENERATE: *From the 16th century word meaning "to beget offspring", from the Latin word generatus, which is the past participle of generare, "to beget, produce"; a set or sequence of items; to create.*

HARDWARE: *The mechanical equipment necessary for conducting an activity*

ILLUSION OF CONTROL: *The tendency to overestimate one's ability to control events.*

IMMEDIATE: *Relating to or existing in the present time.*

INTERDEPENDENCE: *The quality or condition of two or more people (or things) being reliant on each other.*

LEVERAGE: *Gaining opportunity or advantage through the exertion of position, power or influence*

MANAGED ADAPTIVE DECLINE (MAD): *Blindly adapting to unfavorable conditions in a well-managed manner that initially appears to mitigate disruption but quickly accelerates destructive decline.*

MEGA, MACRO AND MICRO SCALES: *The different scales used to identify conditions impacting an organization – the mega (global), the macro (where sector, regional and national forces play out), and the micro level (the space you and your organization occupy).*

MOORE'S LAW: *The observation in 1965 by Intel co-founder Gordon Moore that the number of transistors per square inch on integrated circuits had doubled every year since the invention of the integrated circuit and would continue to do so (at a slowing pace) into the foreseeable future. As of 2015 the pace of change is now at about 2.5 years.*

NEGLECT OF PROBABILITY: *The tendency to completely disregard probability when making a decision under uncertainty.*

NETFLIXED: *Saul Kaplan's description of the outcome of disintermediation and a failed business model.*

OPPORTUNITY: *A set of conditions that provides for progress.*

OPPORTUNITY-RISK: *A set of conditions providing for progress and exposure to danger.*

ORGANIZATIONAL ECOSYSTEM: *The system of systems or network of networks in which an organization resides.*

ORIENTED: *To be aligned to a particular direction or position.*

PRECEPT: *A general rule intended to regulate behavior or thought.*

PROCESSES: *Ways of doing things.*

RAW INPUTS: *Materials, energy, etc. that can be used to build and develop additional capabilities.*

RECIPROCITY: *A virtuous cycle of value generation.*

RESILIENCE (CONVENTIONAL): *To bounce back from shocks or push through adverse conditions.*

RESILIENT FUTURE: *A future where people, organizations and communities – as a whole – change ahead of change.*

RESILIENT FUTURES: *The organization and network of people that author, steward, teach and facilitate the SiA Framework.*

RESILIENT ORGANIZATION: *An organization that changes ahead of change thus avoiding and/or leveraging shocks and adverse events.*

RISK: *A set of conditions providing exposure to danger.*

SCALE: *Proportional dimensions that reduce or increase in size.*

SOFTWARE: *Information and online technology systems and computer programs. Any set of machine-readable instructions that directs a computer's processor to perform specific operations.*

SIA: *See – Strategy in Action.*

SIA ALGORITHM: *The five precepts or steps of Strategy in Action.*

SIA VALUE EQUATION: *The diversity of factors that need to be valued before realizing sustainable financial gain (e.g. the environment, human resources, and value network).*

SOR: *See - Strategic Opportunity-Risk.*

STRANDED ASSETS: *Assets that have suffered from unanticipated or premature write-downs, devaluations or conversion to liabilities.*

STRANDED CAPABILITIES: *Assets that are no longer able to perform a useful function in generating sustainable value.*

STRATEGY IN ACTION: *Strategy that is directly linked and in sync with action, and vice versa.*

STRATEGIC OPPORTUNITY-RISK (SOR): *Opportunity-risk that will strategically position the organization to generate sustainable value.*

SUSTAINABLE VALUE: *Value that persists over time and throughout continuous and discontinuous events.*

SUSTAINABLE VALUE GENERATION: *The ability to continuously understand what is valued and deliver and capture that value over time.*

SYNERGY: *The interaction of elements that when combined produce a total effect that is greater than the sum of its individual parts.*

SYSTEM: *A set of interacting or interdependent components forming an integrated whole.*

SYSTEMIC: *Something that is spread throughout, system-wide, affecting a group or system, such as a body, economy, market or society as a whole.*

TECHNOLOGY: *The collection of tools, including machinery, modifications, arrangements and procedures used by humans; the application of knowledge for practical ends.*

UNFAIR ARBITRAGE: *Where one party bears the entire risk or greater proportion of a risk, and the related opportunity is enjoyed by another party.*

TRUST: *A firm belief in the reliability, truth, or ability of someone or something.*

VALUE: *The importance, worth or usefulness of something; the material or monetary worth of something.*

VALUE DESTRUCTION: *The degradation or loss of value.*

VALUE GENERATION: *To deliver value to others or capture value for yourself.*

VALUE PARTNER: *A person, employee, organization or community who combines with others to share value and together generate sustainable value.*

VALUE PROPOSITION: *The stated value than an organization proposes to deliver to external value partners and capture internally.*

VALUES: *Principles or standards of behavior; one's judgment about what is important in life; the ideals, customs, institutions, etc., of a society toward which the people of a group have an affective regard.*

WILDCARD: *An unexpected event with uncertain qualities and unpredictable outcomes.*

WHOLE SYSTEM: *A nested system of systems; a network of networks.*

SELECTED SOURCES

CHAPTER ONE
Welcome to the Wake-Up: Living in an Exponentially Accelerating Age

1. Loyd, Tony. "The Pace of Change in the VUCA World", vucabook.com/tag/pace-of-change.

2. Bürkner, Hans-Paul. "Globalization: Are You Ready?" Boston Consulting Group, May 2, 2012, www.bcgperspectives.com/content/commentary/globalization_growth_globalization_are_you_ready.

3. Schumpeter, Joseph. Capitalism, Socialism, and Democracy, 1942. Reprinted by Routledge, 2006.

4. Holling, C. S. "Resilience of ecosystems; local surprise and global change." pp. 292-317 in Sustainable Development of the Biosphere, W. C. Clark and R. E. Munn, editors. Cambridge University Press, 1986.

CHAPTER TWO
Thinking SiA: An Algorithm for Strategy at the Speed of Disruption

1. Banks, Russell. The Reserve. Harper Perennial, 2008.

2. McChrystal, Stanley. Team of Teams: New Rules of Engagement for a Complex World. Portfolio, 2015.

3. Quick, Larry with Denny Sterley: Creating Opportunity Ahead of Complex Change. Resilient Futures, 2012.

CHAPTER THREE
What Condition Are My Conditions In?: Learning To Take the Temperature of a Changing World

1. Roubini, Nouriel. IMF Seminar: "The Risk of a U.S. Hard Landing and Implications for the Global Economy and Financial Markets." Transcript, 2007, http://www.imf.org/external/np/tr/2007/tr070913.htm

2. Shtulman, Andrew & Valcarcel, J. "Scientific knowledge suppresses but does not supplant earlier intuitions". Cognition, 2012.

CHAPTER FOUR
Heads or Tails?: Pursuing Strategic Opportunity-Risks

1. "A Steve Jobs' Moment That Mattered: Macworld," August 1997. Posted by Forbes, www.youtube.com/watch?v=EauGoACmp7E.

2. Wolf, Gary. "Steve Jobs: The Next Insanely Great Thing". Wired, 1995.

CHAPTER FIVE
The Bottom-Line & Beyond: Generating Sustainable Value

1. "An interview with John Mackey, founder of Whole Foods", Grist, December 18, 2004, http://grist.org/article/little-mackey.

2. "Declaration of Interdependence", Whole Foods, wholefoodsmarket. com/mission-values/core-values/declaration-interdependence.

3. "Our Core Values", Whole Foods, http://www.wholefoodsmarket. com/mission-values/core-values.

4. Kaplan, Saul. The Business Model Innovation Factory. Wiley, 2012.

5. "Is your business model safe without Integrated Reporting? Interview with Unilever", PWC, www.pwc.com/gx/en/audit-services/corporate-reporting/integrated-reporting/interview-with-unilever-why-is-integrated-reporting-important.jhtml.

CHAPTER SIX
The Right Stuff: Capabilities for Making it All Come to Life

1. "Amplify Mentor Event: Marc Tarpenning (Tesla)", Posted by Jeff Solomon, www.youtube.com/watch?v=hf15nMnayXk.

2. Vance, Ashlee. Elon Musk: Tesla, SpaceX, and the Quest for a Fantastic Future. Harper, 2015.

CHAPTER SEVEN
Power Up: Catalytic Actions for Exponential Growth

1. "#PowerUp The Back Bay", Uber Boston, March 15, 2012, uberbos.tumblr.com/post/19348184497/powerup-the-back-bay.

2. Kalanick, Travis. "Chicago—Uber's Biggest Launch To Date?", Uber, September 22, 2011, newsroom.uber.com/chicago/2011/09/chicago-ubers-biggest-launch-to-date.

3. Gross, Bill. "The Single Biggest Reason Why Startups Succeed", Transcript, 2015. www.ted.com/talks/bill_gross_the_single_biggest_reason_why_startups_succeed/transcript?language=en.

4. Macmillan, Douglas. "Uber Boss: Surge Pricing Is Here To Stay." Wall Street Journal, January 7, 2014. www.wsj.com/articles/SB10001424052702304887104579306622013546350

CHAPTER EIGHT
SiA Revolution: Strategy, Humanity, and Community

1. "Steve Sasson, Digital Camera Inventor", Posted by Kodak Moments, www.youtube.com/watch?v=wfnpVRiiwnM.

ACKNOWLEDGEMENTS

A list so long it could be a book in itself. So, thank you to all of the many people from around the world who, in the past twenty years have supported this work.

In particular ... our fantastic Canadian colleague, researcher, wordsmith and editor Kristin van Vloten. Where would we be without you?

To our many clients throughout the years and especially Jane Grover, Jonathan Tribe, "Abby Harris", Jane Monk, Andrew Wilson-Annan, David Murray, Chris Carroll, Rohan Stocker, Bishop Geoff Smith, Jim Gard'ner, Peter Dawkins, Terry Blake, Greg Blatch, Shelley Pike, Claire Hamilton, Mike Shearer, James Best and Gary Fitzgerald.

To our Australian crew: Paul Szymkowiak, Andrew Hynson, Jennifer Dean, and our Chair, Todd Davies.

And colleagues: Peter Vawdrey, John Kumnick, Bob Grey, Ron Campbell, Denny Sterley, Ben Foskett, Ray Minniecon, Sally Burgess de Castillo, Mal Bryce, Stephen Quinton, Christopher Bell, Damien Pontifex, Helen Allison, Ian Parker, Mike Berry, Grant Symons, David Brown, Peter Ellyard, Laurie Sparke, Jack Carlsen, David Waddell, Chris Jones, Derek Gonsalves, Janette King, Stacey Daniel,

Richard Keeves, Brendan Underwood, Nigel Hayward, Ralph Stevenson and Gary Bourne.

A big thank you to our American supporters too numerous to mention but whom we must acknowledge: Rodgers Frantz, Kip Bergstrom, Fred Presley, Robert Leaver, Peter Kageyama, Kenneth Payne, Ariana McBride, Beth Ashman Collins, Michelle Gonzalez, Jeffrey (Deckers) Deckman, Liz Smith, Buff Chase, Charlie Cannon, Richard Davis, Sharon Conard-Wells, Derek Winslow, Robert Billington, Natalie Carter, Russ Preston, Ramon Martinez, Curt Spalding, Bruce Vild, Kevin Flynn, Virginia Lee, Jen McCann, Jeff Seemann, Babette Allina, Barnaby Evans, Ina Anderson, Rob Allen, Maia Small, The Armory Revival bunch, Cliff Wood, John Speck, Barnaby Evans, Jane Austin, Garry Bliss, Umberto Crenka, John C. Gregory, Paul Ouellette, Paula Watt, Barbara Fields, Ames Colt, Gary Calvino, Richard Henken, Margaux Morisseau, Louis Soares, Justin Aina, Rick Pace, Bill Foulkes, Celeste M. Johnson, Bill Gordon, Geoff Teed, Michelle Bauer, John Englehart, Daniel DiSantis, Bill Bulick, Kimberley Finn, Deb Talbot, Lisa Mansell, and the Tampa Bay gang ... and the inimitable, Mark Binder (who gifted us the name, Resilient Futures).

To Kip Bergstrom, John Howkins, Charles Landry, Charlie Leadbeater, Paul Houghton, Richard Hames, Carol Coletta, David Smith, Michael Shuman, Christopher Alexander, Richard Florida, Joseph Cortwright, Paul Duggan, Daryl Taylor, Ken Standfield, Craig Miller, Peter Morris, Margaret Wheatley, Elliott Washor, Doc Litke, Ken Ford, Michael Mehaffy, Graeme Pearman, John Seely-Brown and Saul Kaplan - a big thanks for your insights.

To our fantastic designer, Najdan Mancic from Iskon Design in New York. A huge thank you for your wonderful talents.

Last but not least ... love and thanks to... the Quick McBack family. Helen, for always being there for me in this twenty-year quest. Ben, James, Anthony, Kylie, Joe and Jason, their wonderful partners and our beautiful grandchildren. Julie, thank you for being in our lives. Mum and dad, bro Ken and my wonderful sister Dee (I wouldn't have been here to author this book with out you Sis) - the first 18 years were all your fault. All at the Sir Charles Gairdner Hospital, Perth ... and Dr. Andrew Wei and Dr. Sharon Avery and all at The Alfred, Melbourne – thank you for my life.

And the Platt family – Simone, Mia and Sophie – my three amazing girls. I do know how lucky I am. To Josh, Lauren, Jordan and Colin and mum. Thank you all for your unending support and love. And to dad – always missed, never forgotten.

ABOUT THE AUTHORS

Larry Quick is a strategist with significant global experience in both the corporate and civic sectors. He is the founder of Resilient Futures and the original developer of the Resilient Futures' Strategy in Action framework. Larry has designed, led, and facilitated countless strategic programs that draw upon his expertise in corporate strategy, innovation, economic development, technology strategy, sustainability and resilience, and urban planning. He is a cancer survivor and is "committed to squeezing every ounce of life that this great world can bring". Larry lives in Woodend, Victoria with his wife Helen.

David Platt is a strategist and expert facilitator with significant experience in the education and social enterprise sectors, community development and resilience. He has designed and led learning experiences that build strategic capability in leaders of organizations across Australia and the United States. When the American-born David is not commuting to Melbourne, he lives in Perth, Western Australia, with his wife and two children.

ABOUT RESILIENT FUTURES

Resilient Futures is a network of strategists, risk managers, analysts and coaches. Strategy In Action (SiA) is the strategic planning framework they created to help organizations leverage—rather than fall prey to—the exponentially accelerating disruptive changes transforming all industries in all sectors, globally.

Resilient Futures helps leaders and teams to re-set their strategic thinking so they can confidently and actively pursue the opportunities and mitigate and manage risks inherent in this era of disruptive change. SiA equips all levels of the organization with a shared language and a common strategic framework allowing strategy - in action - to permeate the whole organization from boardroom to 'coalface,' in sync with change.

SERVICES & LEARNING OPPORTUNITIES

Teams and leaders can learn and implement the SiA framework through:

- this non-fiction book, *Disrupted: Strategy For Exponential Change*
- the training manual, *SiA Study Guide*
- customized organizational training programs through the *SiA: Program Pathway*
- online programs for individuals and teams

CONTACT RESILIENT FUTURES

For more information or to purchase Resilient Futures publications, visit: www.resilientfutures.com

To receive the Resilient Futures Newsletter, email network@resilientfutures.com

For contact email: info@resilientfutures.com
Twitter: #disrupted

Lightning Source UK Ltd.
Milton Keynes UK
UKOW04f0247231015

261177UK00001B/2/P